# SPIDERS
## of Australia

T0342942

## Volker W. Framenau
## and Melissa L. Thomas

First published in 2018 by Reed New Holland Publishers
Sydney

Level 1, 178 Fox Valley Road, Wahroonga, NSW 2076, Australia

newhollandpublishers.com

A record of this book is held at the National Library of Australia.

ISBN 978 1 92554 603 3

Managing Director: Fiona Schultz
Publisher and Project Editor: Simon Papps
Designer: Andrew Davies
Production Director: Arlene Gippert
Printed in China

All images by Volker W. Framenau except for the following: Bryce McQuillan, pages
66, 108, 109 (bottom), 141 (both), 142, 145, back cover; Paul Zborowski, pages 6, 24
(right), 25, 35, 39 (left), 49, 50 (both), 52, 61, 64, 69, 73, 82, 112, 114, 117, 118, 119,
120 (both), 123, 128 (both), 129 (top two), 130 (both), 131, 132 (bottom), 133 (all),
140, 146, 148, 152, 153, 154, 155, 156, 159, 161 (both), 163, 173, 177, 184; Farhan
Bokhari, pages 3, 28, 44, 125 (bottom), 126 (top); Robert White, pages 29, 115, 165;
Alan Henderson, page 176; David Paul, page 101.

10 9 8 7 6 5 4 3 2

Keep up with Reed New Holland
and New Holland Publishers

f ReedNewHolland

⊙ @NewHollandPublishers and @ReedNewHolland

*Female* Tmarus *(Thomisidae) feeding on* Camponotus *ant.*

# CONTENTS

## SPIDER FAMILIES

### ARANEOMORPHAE – Modern Spiders

## MYGALOMORPHAE – Trapdoor Spiders

*Male* Backobourkia heroine *(Araneidae).*

# INTRODUCTION

## SEPARATING FACT FROM FICTION

*"In the spider-web of facts, many a truth is strangled"*
(attributed to Paul Eldridge).

In the modern world of social media platforms it is often difficult to cut through the hype and determine what is fact and what is fiction. Where spiders are concerned, it is often easy to believe tales that lend credibility to Western culture's underlying attitude towards spiders: they should be feared. This cultural belief is a staple in literature and horror movies, including children's nursery rhymes such as *Little Miss Muffet*. This introductory guide debunks a number of the most popular spider myths, while providing an exciting first insight into the amazingly diverse world of Australian spiders.

## AUSTRALIAN SPIDER FAUNA

When it comes to Australian spiders, we have it all. For example, males in the Jumping Spider genus *Maratus*, similar to peacocks, display extravagantly colourful and elaborate mating dances to entice females. Australians can lay claim to having representatives of the fastest running spiders in the world (the Flatties, Selenopidae). We also managed to put our largest city smack bang in the middle of the range of what is arguably one of the most venomous spiders on Earth, the Sydney Funnel-web Spider. Australia's spider diversity is as enormous as it is unique. The country is currently home to about 3,800 described species of spiders, but scientists estimate that between 5,000 and 12,000 species remain to be formally described.

Geological and climatic conditions shaped Australia's spider fauna. Australia once belonged to the southern supercontinent Gondwana. Therefore, the closest relatives of many Australian spiders are found in South America, Africa, India and New Zealand, in particular for the species of the arid centre and the temperate southern latitudes. But the long isolation of this country together with a lack of any major geological disruptions such as significant glaciation meant that there was plenty of time to evolve a unique fauna. A second origin of Australian spiders is South-East Asia, and here many tropical spiders show affinities to faunas found in Australia's north.

In addition, many non-native spider species have been introduced into this country accidentally by humans. These spiders tend to be closely associated with humans and are commonly found in or around houses and include, for example, the Common Daddy Long-legs. Of course, many of Australia's native spiders can also be found making themselves at home in our towns and cities. Arguably no house is without a Black or Brown House Spider despite the human residents' efforts to get rid of them.

## WHAT IS A SPIDER?

Spiders are part of a taxonomic class known as Arachnida. This group also includes scorpions, mites, ticks and some lesser well-known orders such as short-tailed whipscorpions. Amongst the

*Female* Clubiona *(Clubionidae) in silken brood-chamber.*

characters distinguishing spiders from all other arachnids, such as two major body parts divided by a narrow link, the pedicel, the ability to produce silk is arguably the most prominent.

Spider silk is produced within glands inside the second part of the spider's body, the abdomen, and exuded using spinnerets at the end of the body. The spinnerets are armed with a variety of gland spigots that produce many different types of silk with differing mechanical properties and purposes. The best-known use of silk in spiders is for the construction of a web. A spider's web can consist of a number of different silk types, including temporary spirals used in construction, threads to fix the web and either sticky or fuzzy catching threads. Spiders also use silk as safety- or drag-lines, for the lining of burrows, protection of eggs and aerial dispersal of hatchlings via ballooning. This diversity in the types and uses of silk is thought to be key to the success of spiders and their ability to inhabit almost all terrestrial habitats, from coastal regions to the highest mountains and from deserts to tropical rainforests.

The front section of a spider's body is known as the cephalothorax which bears the eyes, mouthparts and legs. Most spiders have eight eyes; however, some have six or less. Eyeless spiders are found in subterranean environments and are particularly prominent in Australia, but they do not feature in this book as they often require specialised collecting equipment (for more comprehensive coverage of Australia's spider fauna see *A Guide to the Spiders of Australia* by Volker W. Framenau, Barbara C. Baehr and Paul Zborowski, published by Reed New Holland, ISBN 978 1 92151 724 2). The number and arrangement of a spider's eyes is particularly important for family-level identification.

# FORAGING AND FEEDING

Many birds prey on spiders, but it is less known that some spiders will eat birds or other vertebrates. Australian spiders are particularly good at catching small vertebrates; the Golden Orb-weavers, Redback Spiders and Australian Tarantulas are regularly found eating lizards, frogs and birds. However, their typical food includes insects, slaters and other spiders. Whilst most species are generalist predators, many species do specialise on particular food groups. Australia is the country of ants, and many spiders exploit this by preying on them. The Ant-eating Spiders (family Zodariidae) are particularly diverse, and expert ant exploiters also include Crab Spiders (genus *Amyciaea*), Jumping Spiders (e.g. genus *Myrmarachne*) and Comb-footed Spiders (genus *Euryopis*).

Spiders are probably best known for capturing their prey in webs, but they have developed many other ingenious ways of putting dinner on the table. In Australia, the most remarkable foraging strategies include throwing a sticky thread at prey (Bola Spiders in the genus *Ordgarius*) or actively throwing a silken net (Net-casting Spiders, family Deinopidae). The Spitting Spiders (genus *Scytodes*) catch their prey by spitting a fluid that consists of venom, silk and a glue-like substance. In contrast, many ground-dwelling or burrowing spiders don't use silk at all to capture their prey, instead they ambush and kill their prey using their legs and powerful fangs.

# LIFE CYCLE

A spider transitions through three life stages: egg, spiderling and adult. Depending on species, female spiders deposit from less than

*Female* Venatrix pullastra *(Lycosidae) carrying eggsac.*

a handful to several thousand eggs into an eggsac. Eggsacs come in all shapes, sizes and colours and are constructed from specialised silk. Many species of spiders will secure one or more eggsacs in a location that is well protected and provide no further care (e.g. many Orb-weaving Spiders, Araneidae). Other species guard their eggsacs until the spiderlings emerge (e.g. many Huntsman Spiders, Sparassidae). Mobile brood care is not uncommon. Female Daddy Long-legs (Pholcidae) and Fishing Spiders (Pisauridae) carry their eggsacs between their jaws, while Wolf Spider (Lycosidae) mothers carry their eggsac fixed to the spinnerets.

When spiderlings emerge from the eggsac they generally look similar to the adult spider, and in most cases they have to fend for themselves. However, there are some instances where brood

*Male of undescribed species in the* Araneus talipedatus *group (Araneidae).*

care for spiderlings occurs. Wolf Spider mothers carry the young on their back for some time before they disperse. Some species are subsocial, living amongst a network of extended family – e.g. Australian Social Huntsman Spider (*Delena cancerides*), some Crab Spiders, Thomisidae (e.g. *Tharrhalea ergandros*) and House Spiders, Desidae (*Phryganoporus candidus*).

Spiders grow by going through a series of moults. Very small spiderlings may moult every few days, but as they get larger in size, the interval between moults can increase to several weeks. The number of moults depends on the ultimate body size. Small spiders will only need a few moults, whereas larger spiders will pass through more than ten moults before reaching the adult stage. As males are often smaller than females they reach maturity earlier, and some of them may guard immature females from rival males in order to be first on the scene when she matures.

Male and female spiders can generally not be distinguished as juveniles. From their penultimate stage (the last stage before moulting to adulthood) spiders begin to form the genital organs, which in males, unique amongst arthropods, includes pedipalps modified into secondary sexual organs. These look like miniature 'boxing gloves' projecting out from the front of the spider. Males use their pedipalps to transfer sperm from their sperm glands under the abdomen to the female genitalia, the epigyne, which is also situated under the abdomen, via a specialised sperm transfer web. The male pedipalp and the female epigyne act like a lock and key mechanism whereby only the male of one species is generally able to fit his pedipalps into the epigyne of a female of the same species. It is not surprising then, that male and female reproductive organs are extremely important in the classification of spiders.

Most male spiders have rather short lives and generally die soon after copulation. In contrast, females usually live much longer because they must care for their brood. Females of some species will mate with multiple males and/or lay multiple eggsacs during their adult life. Females of the Giant Spiny Trapdoor Spider (*Gaius villosus*) have been recorded to live for more than 40 years in natural environments, assisted by the ability of Trapdoor Spiders (Mygalomorphae) to moult after maturation. In contrast, Modern Spiders (Araneomorphae) are generally not able to moult when adult and their adult lifespan is much shorter, generally 1–2 years.

# SPIDER VENOM

Almost all spiders use venom to overcome their prey (or in defence), with the exception of the Venomless Spiders (family Uloboridae) and some other cryptic smaller groups. However, only two Australian spider species have been directly linked to human fatalities, the Redback Spider (*Latrodectus hasseltii*) and the Sydney Funnel-web Spider (*Atrax robustus*). No deaths have occurred since antivenom became available for both species. Curiously, in Redback Spiders, only females are large enough to penetrate human skin; in contrast, it is only the male Sydney Funnel-web Spider venom that has the compound which is dangerous to humans. Many relatives of the Sydney Funnel-web Spider (members of the genera *Atrax* and *Hadronyche* in the family Hexathelidae) occur along the east coast of Australia and are potentially dangerous, but most live a very cryptic lifestyle and are rarely encountered by humans.

Many other spider species are big enough to inflict a painful bite, but effects are generally restricted to the bite site or include mild systemic effects such as headache or nausea as indicated in the species descriptions. Secondary bacterial infections are most likely the cause of major skin lesions sometimes attributed to certain species such as the White-tailed Spider (*Lampona cylindrata*) or the Black House Spider (*Badumna insignis*), as the venom of these spiders does not contain any compound that has the ability to cause such damage. The bite effects of many Australian spiders are unknown, plainly because they are either too small to penetrate human skin or tend to be rarely aggressive.

Information on the effect of a spider's bite or venom are only included in this book if of medical relevance. No medical advice is

*Female* Venatrix lapidosa *(Lycosidae) feeding on juvenile of the same species.*

given; we are arachnologists, not doctors. It is recommended to seek medical advice when bitten. If you manage to capture the culprit, it should be identified by an expert arachnologist.

## HOW TO OBSERVE SPIDERS

Spiders are everywhere and therefore observing them can be easy. There are many species of spiders that you are likely to encounter more regularly in or around the house than in their natural environment. These synanthropic spiders include Daddy Long-legs (Pholcidae), Black House Spiders (Desidae), White-tailed Spiders (Lamponidae) and Redback and Cupboard Spiders (both Theridiidae). Garden Orb-weavers (Araneidae) may build their nocturnal orb-webs on a clothes line and hide in the washing during the day.

*Female* Araneus eburneiventris *(Araneidae) spotted at night.*

Many spiders are initially detected by their web, which attracts the observer to look for its inhabitant. These include the Orb-weaving Spiders (Araneidae), Comb-footed Spiders (Theridiidae), House Spiders (Desidae) and Venomless Spiders (Uloboridae). Crab Spiders are best found by investigating flowers and, similarly, Jumping Spiders can be observed as free-hunters in vegetation or on rock faces and walls.

Most spider species are nocturnal and hide during the day. If you want to find them during daylight hours, the best method is to turn over rocks and logs and pull off the bark of trees. Other successful methods include sieving leaf litter for small ground-dwelling spiders or using an insect net to swipe through vegetation.

Our favourite method for spider-hunting is to grab a torch and venture out at night. Wolf Spider eyes will reflect a greenish-blue light and are therefore easy to locate. Similarly, Huntsman Spider eyes will reflect light, however, unlike the ground-dwelling Wolf Spiders, they will primarily be found at height on trees or in shrubs. Many Orb-weaving Spiders are nocturnal and will renew their web every night. The highly focused beam of a torch will invariably lead to many interesting discoveries on how these spiders construct their delicate web and overcome their food, or one might even see them mating.

Spiders that live in burrows can be very difficult to observe. Some burrow-dwellers stay well hidden behind trapdoors. They build these trapdoors with silk and conceal them with dirt, making their burrows almost undetectable. These spiders only emerge to ambush prey that passes close to their tunnel entrance. Burrows of other spiders, like funnel-webs, are easier to find. These spiders use a series of irregular silk trip-lines radiating out from the burrow entrance to alert the spiders to prey walking nearby. These spiders can sometimes be found foraging close to the tunnel entrance at night.

## THE SPECIES IN THIS BOOK

While this book aims to cover some of the most common species of Australian spiders, there is necessarily some bias towards the authors' places of residence (Vic, WA) and favourite groups of spiders. Wolf Spiders (Lycosidae) and Orb-weaving Spiders (Araneidae) belong to the most commonly encountered groups in the field and are strongly represented here; incidentally, the senior author has studied these groups in detail for more than two decades.

*Male* Missulena granulosa *(Actinopodidae).*

Species are ordered in the two major lineages of Australian spiders, the Araneomorphae (Modern Spiders) and Mygalomorphae (Trapdoor Spiders). Within these groups, families and then species within families are ordered alphabetically by their scientific name.

The common names given in this guide are a combination of generally accepted names (i.e. Redback Spider), and where one of these doesn't exist, a combination of those found in other publications or simply chosen by the authors. In contrast to the scientific name, there is no rule governing common names and there might be local or regional differences for these.

Scientific species names are listed with the person who described the species and year of description. The latter are in parentheses if the species has been placed in a different genus since its original description, following the International Code of Zoological Nomenclature.

The 'ID' part for each species account concentrates on those characters visible in the field and does not include characters of higher taxonomic levels. However, we sometimes give information on similar species or, if applicable, note that very little is known about the taxonomy of a specific group. For some spiders we have not included a particular species, but refer to a number of species in a genus (abbreviated 'spp.' – species). These are generally impossible to identify in the field and/or are taxonomically poorly known.

Often, there are distinct differences between the sexes in spiders, but not always both sexes are illustrated. Where there are differences, these are alluded to in the text. Indeed, many Australian species are currently known only from one sex and there is a lot of work to do to find or match up its counterpart.

The 'Ecology' part of each species description includes what we generally know about the spider's specific habitat preferences, its prey, life cycle or noteworthy behaviours, but in many cases we know preciously little. Very few Australian spider species have been studied in detail.

## LIST OF ABBREVIATIONS USED IN THE SPECIES ACCOUNTS

| ♀ | female | imm | immature |
|---|--------|-----|----------|
| ♂ | male | e.g. | for example |
| ad | adult | c. | circa, approximately |
| juv | juvenile | sp. | species (singular) |

| | | | |
|---|---|---|---|
| spp. | species (plural) | NT | Northern Territory |
| ID | identification | Tas | Tasmania |
| incl | including | NZ | New Zealand |
| NSW | New South Wales | Jan, Feb, Mar, etc | |
| Qld | Queensland | | January, February, |
| WA | Western Australia | | March, etc |
| SA | South Australia | NP | National Park |

*Male* Maratus gemmifer *(Salticidae).*

# THE SPIDERS

## TURRET ORB-WEAVER
*Acroaspis olorina* (Karsch, 1878)

*Female.*

**ID:** Mottled brown with conspicuous turret-shaped abdomen of variable length. Differs from species in genus *Poltys* by closely spaced lateral eyes. ♀ c.8mm, ♂ c.5mm. Many similar undescribed species in genus. ID requires examination under a microscope.

**ECOLOGY:** Builds conventional orb-web at night in open to closed forest. During day, spider sits camouflaged as a little twig on a branch in a tree or shrub.

**RANGE:** South-western WA; other species in genus throughout Australia.

## SCORPION-TAILED SPIDER
*Arachnura higginsii* (L. Koch, 1872)

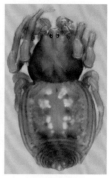

*Female.*

*Male.*

ID: ♀ with elongated abdomen that terminates in multipronged apex. ♂ much smaller than ♀ and abdomen wrinkled. Brown to greenish-cream in colour, juv may be brightly coloured red or yellow. ♀ c.15mm, ♂ c.4mm.

ECOLOGY: Orb-web, often with missing sector, generally near ground in bushland and open woodland. ♀ in web during day. Spiders are autumn-mature in temperate climates.

RANGE: Southern mainland Australia and Tas outside arid centre. In WA, not much further north than Perth; in Qld as far north as Gladstone.

## WHITE-WINGED ORB-WEAVER
*Araneus albotriangulus* (Keyserling, 1887)

*Both images: Female.*

ID: Light triangular marking on abdomen that may be reduced to a transverse line. ♀ c.5mm, ♂ c.3mm. Similar species with more localised distributions in Qld, NSW and Tas. Misplaced in *Araneus* (represents an undescribed Australian genus).

ECOLOGY: Small orb-web with signal line leading to a retreat in a variety of vegetated habitats. Summer-mature in temperate climates.

RANGE: Eastern Australia from Daintree NP, Qld, to Tas.

## SHINY ORB-WEAVER
*Araneus cyrtarachnoides* (Keyserling, 1887)

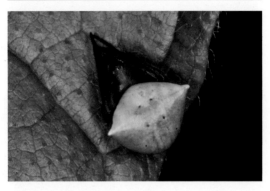

*Female.*

ID: Brown to green with shiny, almost triangular abdomen of very variable colouration, sometimes with white transverse band. ♀ c.5mm, ♂ c.4mm. Misplaced in *Araneus* (represents an undescribed Australian genus).

ECOLOGY: Small orb-web in a variety of vegetated habitats, incl parks and gardens; otherwise ecology poorly known.

RANGE: North-eastern Australia, from about Fraser Island, Qld, into Papua New Guinea.

## BLACK-SHOULDERED ORB-WEAVER
*Araneus dimidiatus* (L. Koch, 1871)

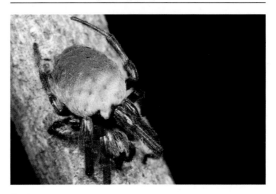

*Female.*

ID: Cream-coloured oval abdomen that has black shoulders and tip. ♀ c.8mm, ♂ c.6mm. Misplaced in *Araneus* (represents an undescribed Australian genus); similar species in genus best identified by colour variations of abdomen.

ECOLOGY: Leaf-curling orb-weaver with vertical orb-web among low vegetation; leaf retreat positioned at top of web frame within a V-shaped open sector of the orb.

RANGE: Eastern Australia, from northern Qld to Vic. Other species in genus with more localised distributions, e.g. *A. mullierarius* in NT and northern Qld.

# GREEN ORB-WEAVER
*Araneus eburneiventris* (Simon, 1908)

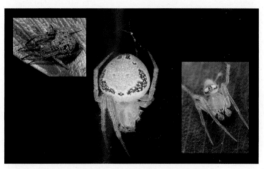

ABOVE: *Typical female.* INSET LEFT: *Black-spotted female.* INSET RIGHT: *Male.*

ID: Overall green with round abdomen that has variable pattern of lines and spots; colour variations unlikely species-specific. ♀ c.6mm, ♂ c.4mm. Misplaced in *Araneus* (represents an undescribed Australian genus). Many species; ID very difficult. Currently described in this genus: *A. circulisparsus* (Keyserling, 1887), *A. ginninderranus* Dondale, 1966, *A. nigropunctatus* (L. Koch, 1871) and *A. psittacinus* (Keyserling, 1887).

ECOLOGY: Very common. Nocturnal. Vertical orb-web in various woodlands, but also suburban parks and gardens.

RANGE: Described from WA, but distribution of this and other species in group unclear due to taxonomic uncertainties.

## SLENDER GREEN ORB-WEAVER
*Araneus talipedatus* (Keyserling, 1887)

*Female.*

ID: Overall green. Elongated abdomen with very variable pattern of white, black and reddish lines and spots. ♀ c.12mm, ♂ c.8mm. Misplaced in *Araneus* (represents an undescribed Australian genus); most common species in genus with about six further undescribed species.

ECOLOGY: Nocturnal orb-weaver with vertical orb-web in various woodlands, but also suburban parks and gardens.

RANGE: Australia south of c.27°S Latitude, from NSW to WA. Other species in this group with generally more localised distribution patterns; these also in Qld.

## OUTSTANDING ORB-WEAVER
*Araneus praesignis* (L. Koch, 1872)

*Female.*

ID: Distinct yellow-and-white abdomen with black transverse lines and two black eye-shaped spots at back. ♀ c.8mm, ♂ c.6mm. Misplaced in *Araneus* (represents undescribed Australian genus); only Australian species in this genus that also includes the Oriental/South-East Asian *A. mitificus* (Simon, 1886) and *Cyclosa bulleri* (Thorell, 1881) from Papua New Guinea.

ECOLOGY: Orb-weaver with vertical orb-web amongst variable vegetation, incl in parks and gardens. Spider rests during day in curled leaf in vegetation.

RANGE: Qld and NSW, from Cape Tribulation in north to approximately Coffs Harbour in south.

## HALF-TAILED ORB-WEAVER
*Araneus senicaudatus* (Simon, 1908)

*Female.*

ID: Variable pale brown to brown in colour with five distinct humps at back of abdomen. Often upper side of abdomen with waved lines along side. ♀ c.15mm, ♂ c.10mm. Misplaced in *Araneus* (represents an undescribed Australian genus). *Eriophora pustulosa* also belongs to this genus.

ECOLOGY: Typical nocturnal orb-weaver with vertical orb-web amongst trees and tall shrubs in open forests and suburban parks and gardens. Ads found in spring and early summer.

RANGE: Most common orb-weaver in south-western Australia. Also occasionally found in SA.

*Male.*

## ST ANDREW'S CROSS SPIDER
*Argiope keyserlingi* Karsch, 1878

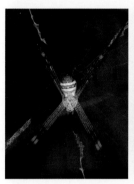 

Female.                              Male.

ID: ♀ with characteristic yellow-and-orange transverse banding on abdomen. ♂ much smaller and inconspicuously coloured. Legs in genus-characteristic cross-shaped position. Can be confused with other similar *Argiope* species, in particular *A. aetherea* (Walckenaer, 1842). ♀ c.15mm, ♂ c.8mm.

ECOLOGY: ♀ sits in web during day. Web with cross-wise decoration in X-orientation believed to attract prey and/or camouflage the spiders. Common in suburban parks and gardens.

RANGE: East coast of Australia from northern Qld to Vic, also on Lord Howe Island and in Tas.

## ELONGATED ST ANDREW'S CROSS SPIDER
*Argiope protensa* L. Koch, 1872

*Female.*

ID: Silvery carapace (as in all *Argiope*) and elongated abdomen that extends beyond spinnerets. Colour variable. Base colour of abdomen silvery-white and often with black or orange longitudinal stripes or bands. ♂ much smaller and inconspicuously coloured. ♀ c.18mm, ♂ c.7mm.

ECOLOGY: ♀ sits in web during day in variable open vegetation; irregular stabilimentum may be present; common in suburban parks and gardens.

RANGE: Throughout Australia; also NZ.

# BANDED GARDEN SPIDER
*Argiope trifasciata* (Forsskål, 1775)

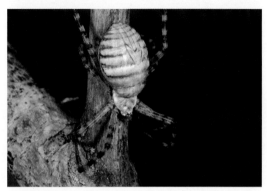

*Female.*

**ID:** Slightly pointed abdomen that has yellow, black and white transverse banding. ♂ much smaller and inconspicuously coloured. ♀ c.18mm, ♂ c.6mm.

**ECOLOGY:** ♀ sits in web during day in variable open vegetation in summer and into autumn. Vertical or irregular stabilimentum may be present. Common in suburban parks and gardens, in particular in south-west and south-east.

**RANGE:** Australia-wide but uncommon in dry interior. Worldwide in temperate and tropical regions.

33

## CHRISTMAS or JEWEL SPIDER
*Austracantha minax* (Thorell, 1859)

*Female.*

ID: Distinct spiny abdomen. Colour variable – most common a stylised white-yellowish V-shaped pattern on black background, but completely black spiders not uncommon. ♂ smaller and spines on abdomen less distinct. ♀ c.9mm, ♂ c.6mm.

ECOLOGY: Very common in all sorts of woody vegetation. Sits in orb-web during day. Threads suspending web adorned with evenly spaced silky fluffy decorations. Webs often in colonies of multiple ♀. Mature spiders generally found from December and into winter months in temperate climates.

RANGE: Australia-wide.  VENOM: Localised minor effects only.

## ORCHARD SPIDER
*Celaenia excavata* L. Koch, 1867

*Female.*

ID: Drawn-out, narrow eye-region (as in all *Celaenia*). Elevated triangular abdomen that imitates bird-dung. When resting legs tightly pressed to body. ♀ c.15mm, ♂ c.5mm.

ECOLOGY: Common in suburban parks and gardens, often in orchards. Only juv constructs web, mature ♀ is nocturnal ambusher and often suspended by a single thread. Attracts moths by imitating their pheromones. The highly camouflaged spiders are best found by looking for their clusters of spherical marbled brown eggsacs.

RANGE: Southern half of Australia, incl Tas; along east coast as far north as Mackay, Qld.

## DESERT ORB-WEAVERS *Backobourkia heroine* (L. Koch, 1871), *B. brounii* (Urquhart, 1885), *B. collina* (Keyserling, 1886)

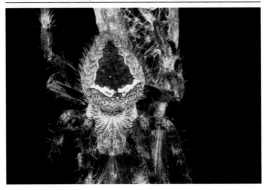

B. heroine *female.*

ID: Variable white triangular mark in front part of abdomen and strong spines on abdomen. Colour very variable. Species in genus  difficult to separate in field and accurate ID requires examination of genitalia under microscope, but overall size and distribution help. *B. heroine* ♀ c.11–25mm, ♂ c.6–15mm. *B. brounii* ♀ c.7–17mm, ♂ c.5–12mm. *B. collina* ♀ c.6–15mm, ♂ c.2–3mm.

B. heroine *female.*

B. heroine *male*.

ECOLOGY: *B. heroine* and *B. brounii* are typical nocturnal orb-weavers with vertical orb-web among trees and large shrubs in open sclerophyll forests, but also gardens and parks. Mature from Sep–May. *B. collina* occurs in the semi-arid and arid centre but also dry coastal heath and grassland. Mature throughout most the of year.

RANGE: *B. heroine* found in southern half of Australia, but less common in east; also in New Caledonia and Norfolk Island.

*B. brounii* found Australia-wide, except far north; also in NZ. *B. collina* found Australia-wide except wetter parts of south-west and south-east.

VENOM: Unknown, possibly minor localised effects by larger spiders.

B. brounii *male*.

## ELONGATED CYCLOSA
*Cyclosa bacilliformis* Simon, 1908

*Male.*

ID: Abdomen elongated and mottled. Carapace of ♀ with pale lateral bands. ♂ much smaller than ♀ and with flat and uniformly dark carapace. ♀ c.12mm, ♂ c.10mm.

ECOLOGY: Spiders found in orb-webs during day and camouflaged by vertical web decorations that include prey remains. Found in open woodland and grassland, incl habitats with grasstrees (*Xanthorrea* spp.)

RANGE: Southern Australia south of 30°S Latitude, incl Tas.

## SOOTY ORB-WEAVER
*Cyclosa fuliginata* (L. Koch, 1872)

*Female.*      *Male.*

ID: Generally mottled brown abdomen and with pattern of longitudinal waved bands; abdomen may have small hump at end. Underside with pair of spindle-shaped white markings. ♀ c.9mm, ♂ c.7mm. Misplaced in *Cyclosa* (represents undescribed Australian genus); genus also includes *Araneus brisbanae* (L. Koch, 1867), *A. recherchensis* Main, 1954 and *A. rubicundulus* (Keyserling, 1887).

ECOLOGY: At night in orb-webs in a variety of vegetation, incl in parks and gardens. During day found in shelter made of folded leaves.

RANGE: Eastern Australia from northern NSW into Vic, also in Tas. *Araneus brisbanae* has similar distribution but also occurs into northern Qld. *Araneus recherchensis* limited to SA and WA.

## THREE-LOBED CYCLOSA
*Cyclosa trilobata* (Urquhart, 1885)

*Female.*

ID: Abdomen with three lobes at back and red longitudinal banding. Carapace of ♀ with deep transverse groove behind head area. ♂ much smaller than ♀ and with flat carapace. ♀ c.10mm, ♂ c.6mm. Similar species in genus include more tropical *C. insulana* (Costa, 1834) and *C. camelodes* (Thorell, 1878).

ECOLOGY: Found in orb-webs in low vegetation during day and camouflaged by prey remains as web decoration. Ads mainly found from Sep–Mar.

RANGE: Australia approximately south of 20°S Latitude. Also in NZ.

## DWARF CYCLOSA *Cyclosa vallata* (Keyserling, 1886), *Cyclosa mulmeinensis* (Thorell, 1887)

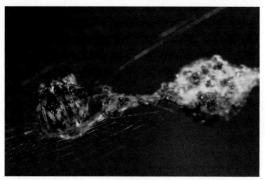

*Female.*

ID: Species complex within *Cyclosa* with mottled spherical abdomen and variable humps at front. ♂ smaller than ♀ and with flat carapace. ♀ c.4mm, ♂ c.3mm. *Araneus apobleptus* Rainbow, 1916, *Carepalxis poweri* (Rainbow, 1916) and *C. lichensis* (Rainbow, 1916) belong in this species complex.

ECOLOGY: Spiders found in orb-webs in low vegetation during day. Spiders camouflaged by prey remains that decorate web in a vertical line.

RANGE: Most common in subtropical and tropical Australia. In NSW as far south as Wollongong.

## PAN-WEB ORB-WEAVER
*Cyrtophora exanthematica* (Doleschall, 1859)

Female.

ID: Overall brown with typical two-pointed abdomen that has two longitudinal white lines. ♂ (as in all *Cyrtophora*) much smaller. ♀ c.10mm, ♂ c.5mm.

ECOLOGY: Messy web in gardens, parks and other well-vegetated habitats.

RANGE: Northern WA, NT and into northern NSW; also on Lord Howe Island and from South-East Asia into India.

# DOME-WEB ORB-WEAVER
*Cyrtophora moluccensis* (Doleschall, 1857)

*Female.*

ID: Abdomen longer than wide and with two distinct shoulder humps. Variably marbled white and orange, red or black. ♂ (as in all *Cyrtophora*) much smaller. ♀ c.20mm, ♂ c.8mm.

ECOLOGY: Tightly meshed dome-shaped web in disturbed or open vegetation in tropical to subtropical climates. May occur in groupings of multiple webs and spiders of different ages.

RANGE: Northern WA, NT and into northern NSW. Also Pacific islands and from South-East Asia into India.

## SOUTHERN TENT ORB-WEAVER
*Cyrtophora parnasia* L. Koch, 1872

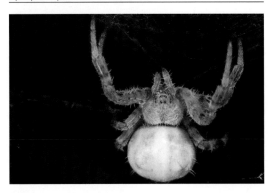

*Female.*

ID: Whitish to pale brown slightly elongated abdomen that may have dark patches at front. Black ring around spinnerets. ♀ c.12mm, ♂ c.5mm.

ECOLOGY: Very tightly meshed dome-shaped web at about 50cm from ground suspended in irregular space-web. Retreat in apex of web made of dry leaves and twigs interwoven with soft silk. Ads most common late summer and into winter.

RANGE: Southern two-thirds of Australia, incl Tas.

## WRAP-AROUND SPIDERS
*Dolophones* spp.

Male.

ID: Abdomen wider than long. Upper side of abdomen highly variable and often elevated into a central turret. ♂ with multiple strong spines on pedipalp tibia. Species-level ID of 17 Australian species currently not possible due to lack of modern taxonomic treatment. ♀ c.8–12mm, ♂ c.6–10mm.

ECOLOGY: All types of woody vegetation, incl forests and bushland. Nocturnal complete orb-web. Spiders hide camouflaged and 'wrapped around' twigs and branches during the day.

RANGE: Australia-wide in all climatic zones; genus otherwise only reported from Indonesia and New Caledonia.

## GARDEN ORB-WEAVER *Eriophora biapicata*
(L. Koch, 1871), *E. transmarina* (Keyserling, 1865)

*Both images: female* E. biapicata.

ID: Highly variable abdomen colouration with white bands, crosses or spots. Species-level ID very difficult in field (impossible in ♂); abdomen of *E. biapicata* may be drawn out into two indistinct tips. ♀ c.15–25mm, ♂ c.10–20mm. Misplaced in *Eriophora* (represents an undescribed Australian genus). This genus also includes *Araneus urbanus* (Keyserling, 1887) and *A. scutigerens* Hogg, 1900.

ECOLOGY: Constructs very large, complete orb-webs at night between trees in open forests, gardens and parks. Webs taken down before dawn. *Eriophora biapicata* mature in late summer to autumn in temperate zones.

RANGE: *Eriophora biapicata* found in all mainland states, incl temperate and arid zones, but rarer towards tropical north and east coast. Here *E. transmarina* dominates and is found from tropical WA, NT and Qld along east coast as far south as about Jervis Bay, NSW.

**VENOM:** Timid and only bite if threatened, for example when hiding in clothes on a washing line during day; bites have generally only minor local effects.

47

# HUMPED ORB-WEAVERS
*Eriophora pustulosa* (Walckenaer, 1842)

*Female.*                                    *Female underside.*

ID: Variable brown colouration and five distinct humps at back of abdomen. Characteristic elongated hourglass-shaped transverse white line under abdomen. ♀ c.15mm, ♂ c.10mm. Misplaced in *Eriophora* (represents an undescribed Australian genus). *Araneus senicaudatus* also belongs to this genus.

ECOLOGY: Nocturnal with vertical orb-web among trees and tall shrubs in open forests and suburban parks and gardens. Ad *E. pustulosa* found throughout year, most commonly in summer.

RANGE: Found in southern half of Australia, incl Tas, with exception of arid centre. Also in NZ.

# FORNICATING SPINY ORB-WEAVER
*Gasteracantha fornicata* (Fabricius, 1775)

*Female.*

ID: Spiny abdomen that is much wider than long and has dark brown traverse bands on white-yellow to turquoise background. Sternum yellow. ♀ c.11mm, ♂ c.3mm.

ECOLOGY: Found during day in orb-webs at about 2m height in vegetation. Otherwise ecology poorly known.

RANGE: Central to northern Qld. Reports of the species outside Australia may be based on misidentifications of similar species.

## REED-SPINNING ORB-WEAVER
*Neoscona theisi* (Walckenaer, 1842)

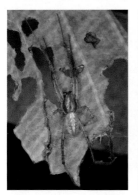

*Male.*  *Female.*

ID: Brown to almost green with distinct dorsal folium pattern on abdomen and dark longitudinal markings on carapace. ♀ c.12mm, ♂ c.10mm.

ECOLOGY: Orb-web in various types of vegetation, around houses and along fences. Nocturnal with spiders in daytime retreat, often a rolled leaf.

RANGE: Tropical to subtropical northern Australia. In Qld as far south as Brisbane, in WA to Shark Bay. Also from India to China and South-East Asia, and on Pacific islands.

## AUSTRALIAN GOLDEN ORB-WEAVER
*Nephila edulis* (Labillardière, 1799)

*Female.*

ID: ♀ with silvery-white carapace and slightly elongated creamy- to purplish-grey abdomen. Differs from similar *N. plumipes* by lack of tubercle on sternum. ♀ up to 35mm; ♂ highly variable in size, c.3–15mm.

ECOLOGY: All climatic zones. Open forests, but also disturbed vegetation such as roadsides, parks and gardens. Large orb-web with golden tinge. Often occurs in aggregations of multiple ♀. Incorporates vertical strands of prey remains into web.

RANGE: Throughout Australia; also New Caledonia, NZ (North Island) and Papua New Guinea.

VENOM: Very unlikely to bite despite size. Bites generally cause local symptoms only, in rare cases nausea and dizziness.

# GIANT GOLDEN ORB-WEAVER
*Nephila pilipes* (Fabricius, 1793)

ID: Silvery-white carapace and variably coloured elongated abdomen, often with longitudinal yellow stripes. Legs black with yellow joints, particularly obvious from underneath. ♀ up to 45mm; ♂ c.3–10mm.

ECOLOGY: Closed tropical and subtropical forests. May catch birds, bats and snakes. Constructs eggsac in depression excavated on forest floor, unlike other species in genus which place it in vegetation.

Female.

RANGE: Mainly coastal, from northern WA into northern NSW. Otherwise known from Asia and western Pacific islands.

VENOM: Bites rare but generally cause local symptoms or pain, redness and swelling. In rare cases nausea and dizziness.

## ORANGE PARAPLECTANOIDES
*Paraplectanoides crassipes* Keyserling, 1886

*Female.*

**ID:** ♀ orange-brown, squat and with flat upper abdomen. Front legs orange-brown, hind legs black. ♂ smaller, black with orange humeral abdominal tips. ♀ c.10mm, ♂ c.3mm.

**ECOLOGY:** Very cryptic spiders that build an ovoid nest in low vegetation such as prostate shrubs or coastal heath and under logs and loose stones. ♀ may live more than 6 years. Prey specialist on springtails and cockroaches.

**RANGE:** Coastal subtropical and temperate Australia from Rockingham, Qld, southwards into WA as far north as Perth; also in Tas.

## GRAEFFE'S LEAFCURLER
*Phonognatha graeffei* (Keyserling, 1865)

*Female.*

ID: Pale brown carapace and legs. Abdomen elongated ovoid with dark opposing C-shaped markings. Similar to *P. melanopyga* (L. Koch, 1871), but lacks black tip of abdomen. ♀ c.13mm, ♂ c.8mm.

ECOLOGY: Incorporates curled leaf into often asymmetrical orb-web, with opening located at hub of snare. Web construction and repair occur during night with spiders hiding in leaf during day. Mate-guarding ♂ often found with ♀ in retreat.

RANGE: Eastern Australia from Townsville, Qld, south into eastern SA; also Tas.

## PALE LEAF-CURLER
*Phonognatha melania* (L. Koch, 1871)

*Female.*

ID: Pale brown carapace and legs. Abdomen elongated ovoid with whitish mottling. ♀ c.10mm, ♂ c.6mm.

ECOLOGY: Open sclerophyll and temperate forests. As with all *Phonognatha* has curled leaf in orb-web. Spiders found outside retreat only at night. Mate-guarding ♂ often found with ♀ in retreat. In south-western Australia, *P. melania* mature from late summer into early winter.

RANGE: Sporadic in eastern Australia (south-eastern Qld, NSW); common in south-western WA.

## ENAMEL SPIDER
*Plebs bradleyi* (Keyserling, 1887)

*Female.*

ID: Elongated, shiny abdomen that generally has stylised orange-red V-shaped pattern. A variety of other colour patterns may be displayed, incl uniformly yellow and green variants. Underside of abdomen with Ü-shaped white marking. ♀ c.12mm, ♂ c.6mm.

ECOLOGY: Orb-web in various vegetation, in open forests and bushland, garden and parks; spider in web during day; mature generally between Sep–Mar.

RANGE: South-eastern Australia (NSW, ACT, Vic, Tas), rare in south-eastern Qld and SA.

# GRASS ORB-WEAVER
*Plebs cyphoxis* (Simon, 1908), *P. eburnus* (Keyserling, 1886)

*Female* P. cyphoxis.

ID: Elongated abdomen and mottled folium-pattern on top, underside with Ü-shaped white marking. ♀ c.8mm, ♂ c.4mm.

ECOLOGY: Low orb-web with vertical decoration mainly in grassy areas in open forests and parks and gardens. In web during day. Ad *P. eburnus* have been found throughout year, but more commonly from summer to late autumn. *Plebs cyphoxis* ad numbers peak between Sep–Nov.

RANGE: *Plebs eburnus* from northern Qld to Tas and into southern SA. *Plebs cyphoxis* in south-western WA and into SA and rare in south-eastern Qld.

# TWO-SPINED SPIDER
*Poecilopachys* spp.

*Female.*

ID: Shiny abdomen with two distinct white, pointy cones. Very colourful in shades of yellow, red, green and black. ♂ much smaller with triangular, very spiny abdomen. Often referred to as a single species, *P. australasia* (Griffith and Pidgeon, 1833), but at least five very similar species occur and their taxonomy is unresolved. ♀ c.8mm, ♂ c.3mm.

ECOLOGY: In orb-web at night in low vegetation. ♀ has been observed to change colour.

RANGE: A number of species mainly along east coast of Australia.

# ROUGH TWIG SPIDER
*Poltys laciniosus* Keyserling, 1886

*Female.*

ID: Dark brown to black carapace. Abdomen mottled grey, higher than long but shape highly variable imitating small branch or twig. As in all *Poltys* lateral eyes widely spaced. In resting position, legs drawn over carapace. ♀ c.9mm, ♂ c.4mm. Eight species of *Poltys* in Australia difficult to separate in field.

ECOLOGY: Nocturnal orb-web in open forest at variable height, spider rests in vegetation during day camouflaged as twig. Moths are a major food item, but other insects taken.

RANGE: Throughout Australia, although possibly absent from dry interior and north-west.

## KARRI FOREST ASSASSIN SPIDER
*Zephyrarchaea janineae* Rix and Harvey, 2012

Female.

**ID**: Elevated head region forming 'neck' with carapace and very long fangs. Abdomen with six paired hump-like tubercles. ♀ c.3.5mm, ♂ c.3mm.

**ECOLOGY**: Elevated leaf litter in wet forested habitats, in particular Karri forest, and coastal groves of Peppermint (*Agonis* spp.). Ads have been found from Apr–Sep. Obligate predators of other spiders, which are speared with elongated chelicerae.

**RANGE**: South-western WA. From Leeuwin-Naturaliste NP and Wellington NP in west to Pemberton in east. Other Archaeidae are cryptic spiders in mesic habitats in south-western Australia and along Great Dividing Range in east.

## HIGH-HEADED ARKYS
*Arkys alticephala* (Urquhart, 1891)

Female.

ID: Elongate rectangular carapace when viewed from above. Abdomen longer than wide and knobbly with central upper tubercle and somewhat constricted on sides. Mottled overall in a variety of brown shades, similar to many other *Arkys* species. ♀ c.7mm, ♂ c.5mm.

ECOLOGY: *Arkys* are thought to be sit-and-wait predators that capture prey by waiting in vegetation with outstretched front legs. Eggsacs built in autumn in vegetation near ground. Juvs hatch before spring.

RANGE: Southern Australia, roughly south of a line from Sydney to Perth.

## WALCKENAER'S TRIANGULAR SPIDER
*Arkys walckenaeri* Simon, 1879

Female.

ID: Orange-red carapace with small protrusions on side of head region. Elongate triangular abdomen with darker marbled red, black and white pattern, but less distinct patterns occur. Similar to *Arkys lancearius* Walckenaer, 1837. ♀ c.8mm, ♂ c.7mm.

ECOLOGY: Appears to prefer canopy of eucalypt forests generally above 2.5m. Forages from single, horizontal thread of silk that spans approximately 10–15cm (occasionally longer), where spider rests with extended forelegs. Mature from about Dec–early Feb. Prey includes small flies.

RANGE: Southern Australia, roughly south of line from Sydney to Perth.

# WESTERN DEMADIANA
*Demadiana cerula* (Simon, 1908)

Female

ID: Orange-brown. Carapace with dense punctuations. Abdomen round to subtriangular with orange sigillae on white, marbled background. Similar to other Australian *Demadiana* and ID requires examination of genitalia under a microscope. ♀ c.2mm, ♂ c.2mm.

ECOLOGY: Found suspended on single threads in *Eucalyptus* and *Acacia* trees. Ad generally found between Mar–May, rarely later in year.

RANGE: South-western WA. Other species of *Demadiana* occur throughout southern half of Australia, incl Tas.

## SAC SPIDERS
*Clubiona* spp.

*Female.*

**ID:** Somewhat elongated, but robust and pale brown with variable darker patterns on abdomen. ♀ c.10mm; ♂ c.8mm. Taxonomy of genus *Clubiona* in Australia without modern taxonomic treatment and species-level ID difficult. Currently 18 species recognised, but diversity likely much higher.

**ECOLOGY:** Common nocturnal bark- or litter-dwelling spiders on and under trees and shrubs in variety of vegetation. ♀ deposits eggsac in a silken chamber under bark, in which they stay until juvs hatch.

**RANGE:** Throughout Australia. Species-specific distribution patterns unresolved due to poor taxonomy.

**VENOM:** Mild to strong local pain, redness and swelling.

# WHITE-SPOTTED SWIFT SPIDER
*Nyssus albopunctatus* (Hogg, 1896)

*Female.*

ID: Black with distinct pattern of white spots on carapace and abdomen. Carapace spots in two lines with the last forming an open triangle. Central abdominal pairs of spots decreasing in size towards back. Legs with white annulations. ♀ c.10mm, ♂ c.8mm.

ECOLOGY: Very fast and common runners in open forested habitats in all Australian climatic zones. Appears to mimic mutilid wasps (velvet ants).

RANGE: Australia-wide, incl Tas. Introduced to NZ.

VENOM: Localised effects like pain, redness and swelling.

CORINNIDAE

## COMMON SWIFT SPIDER
*Nyssus coloripes* (Walckenaer, 1805)

*Female.*

**ID:** Black with distinct central and lateral white lines on carapace. Abdomen with characteristic pattern of white or orange lines and spots, the two central of which are in a pair. Two frontal leg pairs often with orange-brown colouration. Legs with white annulations. ♀ c.10mm; ♂ c.8mm.

**ECOLOGY:** Very fast and common runners in open habitats, incl unvegetated river banks, grassland and open forests and bushlands in all climatic zones. Part of a mimicry chain that also includes cherid beetles (*Tragodendron fasciculatum*) and spider wasps (Pompilidae).

**RANGE:** Australia-wide, incl Tas. Introduced to NZ.

**VENOM:** Localised effects like pain, redness and swelling.

# GREEN-HEADED ANT-MIMIC
*Poecilipta smaragdinea* Simon, 1909

*Female.*

ID: Spectacularly coloured spider with iridescent blue-green carapace that is covered with white spots. Abdomen metallic brown with rusty transverse bands. ♀ c.5mm; ♂ c.5mm.

ECOLOGY: Ecology poorly known. Found in a variety of temperate and semi-arid vegetated habitats, where roams freely and hunts for prey. Most specimens collected between Apr–Jun, suggesting an autumn- to winter-mature species.

RANGE: South-western WA.

## NET-CASTING SPIDER
*Deinopis subrufa* L. Koch, 1879

*Both images: male.*

ID: Variably brown with enlarged posterior median eyes. Elongate abdomen often has longitudinal dark banding. Carapace often with elongated Y-shaped white pattern. Legs very long. ♂ pedipalps with long, coiled embolus. ♀ c.23mm, ♂ c.18mm.

ECOLOGY: Forest habitats, but also in high grass, trees and shrubs in parks and gardens. Active at night supported by extremely powerful eyesight. Hunts near ground suspended on single thread by throwing a cribellate net held between two first pairs of legs over passing prey. Eggsacs spherical and marked with black spots, often in clusters suspended from twigs or in grass.

RANGE: Throughout Australia, less common in interior.

# BLACK HOUSE SPIDER
*Badumna insignis* (L. Koch, 1872)

*Female.*

ID: Carapace and legs black. Abdomen dark grey often with lighter markings. ♀ c.18mm, ♂ c.15mm. Similar to Grey House Spider (*B. longiqua*) (L. Koch, 1867) which is smaller and paler with a grey carapace and brown legs.

ECOLOGY: Very common in houses, where builds messy, cribellate sheet-web that tapers into funnel-shaped retreat in any corner available. Naturally occurs on bark and under rocks and logs. Young can frequent webs for a period without mother showing aggression.

RANGE: Common Australia-wide. More frequent in southern half of country.

VENOM: Bite can be very painful and may cause general malaise such as nausea and vomiting.

## SOCIAL OUTBACK SPIDER
*Phryganoporus candidus* (L. Koch, 1872)

*Female.*

ID: Pale grey to brown with dark, irregular banding in centre of abdomen. ♀ c.8mm, ♂ c. 6mm.

ECOLOGY: Social spider that builds its communal nest in trees or shrubs. Messy nest often incorporates old, dried leaves. It may house hundreds of spiders. Peak colony growth late spring and early summer. Nests are unoccupied in autumn.

RANGE: Common Australia-wide.

## YELLOW or SLENDER SAC SPIDERS
*Cheiracanthium* spp.

*Male.*

**ID:** Elongated, often gracile. Pale brown to greenish, sometimes with darker patterns on carapace and abdomen. ♂ with cymbial spur on pedipalp. ♀ c.9mm, ♂ c.7mm. Taxonomy of genus *Cheiracanthium* in Australia without modern taxonomic treatment, making species-level ID difficult.

**ECOLOGY:** Common bark- and foliage-dwellers in a variety of vegetation. Often in suburban parks and gardens. ♀ deposits eggsac in silken chamber and remains until juvs hatch.

**RANGE:** Throughout Australia in all climatic zones. Species-specific distribution patterns unresolved due to poor taxonomy.

**VENOM:** Local pain and discomfort, redness and itching. Minor skin lesions may occur, but recent investigations showed no evidence of previously suspected dermonecrosis.

## SPECTACULAR GROUND SPIDER
*Ceryerda cursitans* Simon, 1909

*Male.*

ID: Contrasting white (carapace) and creamy (abdomen) patches on black background. Legs black with creamy-white annulations. ♀ c.12mm, ♂ c.8mm. A similar, undescribed species in *Ceryerda* from northern-western Australia has white brushes on front legs, which are lacking in *C. cursitans* ♂.

ECOLOGY: Possibly nocturnal ground-hunting spiders in temperate to semi-arid and arid woodlands and grasslands. Has been found under logs and rocks and in leaf litter.

RANGE: Widespread west of Great Dividing Range, but rarely collected.

## SPOTTED GROUND SPIDERS
*Eilica* spp.

*Female.*

ID: Red or black carapace. Abdomen with white or creamy spots in variety of patterns, often in pairs. Legs black or with reddish pattern. ♀ c.4mm, ♂ c.3mm. Seven Australian species described in *Eilica*, but genus much more diverse.

ECOLOGY: Ground-hunting spiders found in almost every vegetated habitat. Species associated with and/or living in ant colonies, where ants tend to spider clutches, but exact interactions were only sporadically observed. Some *Eilica* appear to feed on ants.

RANGE: Throughout country incl Tas. Species-specific distribution patterns poorly known due to poor taxonomic resolution.

73

# FLATTENED BARK SPIDER
*Hemicloea rogenhoferi* L. Koch, 1875

*Female.*

ID: Very flat, fairly uniform brown. Legs positioned in sideways (laterigrade) fashion. ♀ c.15mm, ♂ c.12mm. Genus *Hemicloea*, which includes 12 described species in Australia, without modern taxonomic treatment.

ECOLOGY: Nocturnal hunters under bark of trees, but also found under rocks and logs. ♀ glues opaque disc-shaped eggsacs under bark and guards them until juvs hatch.

RANGE: *Hemicloea rogenhoferi* is believed to be restricted to eastern Australia; also found in NZ. Other *Hemicloea* species occur throughout Australia in all climatic zones.

# FICKERT'S LONG-SPINNERET BARK SPIDER
*Tamopsis fickerti* (L. Koch, 1876)

*Female.*

ID: Extremely long spinnerets, raised eye area and very long legs. Abdomen with well demarcated dorsal pattern that includes dark narrow heart-mark. Colour tone variable and adjusted to background. Very dark spiders have been found. ♀ c.7mm, ♂ c.5mm.

ECOLOGY: Very common bark-dweller in open forests, garden and parks. Long-spinneret Bark Spiders have specialised hunting method that involves rapidly encircling prey and immobilising it with a layer of silk excreted from movable long spinnerets.

RANGE: South-eastern Australia from approximately Hervey Bay, Qld, to Adelaide, SA; apparently absent in Tas.

75

## COMMON WHITE-TAILED SPIDER
*Lampona cylindrata* (L. Koch, 1866)

*Male.*

**ID:** Dark grey to brown, elongated (more so in ♂) with distinct white spot at end of abdomen. Sometimes four large pale patches in front half of abdomen. ♀ c.18mm, ♂ c.16mm. Indistinguishable in field from slightly smaller *L. murina*.

**ECOLOGY:** Under bark, logs or rocks in forests, also around human habitation. Preys on other spiders. ♀ with eggsac mainly from Sep–Apr.

**RANGE:** Widespread mainly in southern half of Australia. Introduced NZ. Similar *L. murina* mainly along east coast from tropical Qld to Vic.

**VENOM:** Mainly localised pain and minor skin lesions. Sometimes nausea and headaches. No evidence that venom causes necrotic ulcers.

76

## WESTERN FOREST ARTORIA
*Artoria cingulipes* Simon, 1909

*Male.*

ID: Dark brown with pale brown median band on carapace and distinct pale spindle-shaped heart mark on abdomen. ♀ c.7mm, ♂ c.5mm. One of many forest-dwelling species of *Artoria* that can only be identified by examining their genitalia under a microscope.

ECOLOGY: Eucalypt forest and woodlands, incl Jarrah, Marri and Karri forest, where the spiders roam in the ground litter layer. Ad spiders mainly found in spring and summer.

RANGE: Known from WA south of 23°S Latitude and southern SA.

# RIVER ARTORIA
*Artoria mckayi* Framenau, 2002

Female carrying eggsac.                          Male.

ID: Brown with indistinct pale median bands on carapace and abdomen, less distinct in ♀. ♂ pedipalp with distinct white setae at base. ♀ c.6mm, ♂ c.5mm. In Vic can be mistaken for *A. albopedipalpis* Framenau, 2002, with which it shares same habitat. ID requires microscopic examination of genitalia.

ECOLOGY: Hunts freely among rocks at very edge of water on gravelly and sandy river banks.

RANGE: Waterways draining from Great Dividing Range, from central Qld to central Vic; also in Tas. In Vic, ads found throughout year, while ♀ carrying eggsacs only between Nov–Feb.

# POLISHED WOLF SPIDER
*Artoriopsis expolita* (L. Koch, 1877)

*Male.*

ID: Grey carapace, darker in eye region and at back. Abdomen with distinct pale spindle-shaped heart mark that dissects central diamond-shaped black patch. ♀ c.9mm; ♂ c.8mm. Less common *A. klausi* Framenau, 2007 from south-eastern Australia and *A. melissae* Framenau, 2002 from eastern coastal Australia are very similar and ID requires examination of genitalia under microscope.

ECOLOGY: Common in open, moderately moist environments and frequently found near creeks and rivers, in fore dunes, on pasture and suburban lawns. Ad found from Oct–Jan, ♀ with eggsacs during Nov–Dec.

RANGE: Mainland Australia south of 25°S latitude. Also in Tas.

## SERRATED PALISADE WOLF SPIDER
*Dingosa serrata* (L. Koch, 1877)

*Male.*

ID: Distinct pattern includes forked white lines around eyes and serrated dark median band on abdomen. ♀ c.10mm, ♂ c.10mm. Genus *Dingosa* includes four species which are difficult to separate in field.

ECOLOGY: Common on sandy soils of variable humidity in low vegetation, incl behind dunes near ocean. Open burrow 10–20cm deep surrounded by palisade of grass, leaves or pieces of wood. In WA, ad ♀ generally present from May–Nov, mature ♂ from Mar–Apr.

RANGE: Mainland Australia south of 25°S latitude.

## TWO-COLOURED DESERT WOLF SPIDER
*Hoggicosa bicolor* (Hogg, 1905)

ID: ♀ with cream
carapace and black
abdomen with cream
central patch or
variable wide band.
Leg femora black,
but other segments
cream. ♂ indistinct
uniform grey-cream.
♀ c.22mm, ♂ c.16mm.

*Female.*

ECOLOGY: Arid to semi-arid habitats on sandy plains, sometimes
claypans and stony soil between Mulga, Ironwood, chenopods and
spinifex. Can be found in permanent burrows that may be closed
with trapdoor. ♀ mature throughout year; ad ♂ from Aug–Apr.

RANGE: Arid and semi-arid Western and central Australia, into
western Qld;
currently not known
from NSW, Vic or
Tas.

*Male.*

81

# FORREST'S WOLF SPIDER
*Hoggicosa forresti* (McKay, 1973)

*Female.*

**ID:** ♀ with cream carapace and abdomen. Abdomen with black heart mark. Leg femora black with upper basal cream marking, remainder of leg cream. ♂ uniformly grey-brown. ♀ c.22mm, ♂ c.16mm.

**ECOLOGY:** Prefers gritty, stony and fine clay loams, as well as sandplains. Found in woodlands of Gimlet and Salmon Gum as well as Mallee and Spinifex. Ad ♀ found year-round and ad ♂ from Nov–May. Excavates burrows armed with trapdoor.

**RANGE:** Central and southern WA and southern SA.

## STORR'S WOLF SPIDER
*Hoggicosa storri* (McKay, 1973)

*Female.*

ID: ♀ with pale brown to cream carapace and black abdomen. Leg femora cream, patella and tibiae black and metatarsi and tarsi white. ♂ uniformly brown. ♀ c.22mm, ♂ c.16mm.

ECOLOGY: Arid to semi-arid habitats on sandy plains, sometimes claypans and stony soil between Mulga, Ironwood, chenopods and spinifex. Found in permanent burrows that may be closed with trapdoor. ♀ mature throughout year, ad ♂ from Aug–Apr.

RANGE: Arid and semi-arid WA and possibly western SA south of 25°S Latitude.

## CURL-FOOTED WOLF SPIDER
*Hogna crispipes* (L. Koch, 1877)

*Male.*

**ID:** Brown carapace with pale median and lateral bands, the latter incl three dark spots along carapace margins. Underside uniformly pale brown. ♀ c.22mm; ♂ c.16mm.

**ECOLOGY:** Apparently widespread. Very common in open habitats near any water source, including coasts, where it roams freely hunting invertebrate prey.

**RANGE:** Throughout mainland Australia, not reported from Tas; found from Christmas Island (Indian Ocean) into the Pacific (incl NZ), possibly as far as Hawai'i.

**VENOM:** Bite can cause local effects only, such as redness and minor swelling.

# TRIANGLE WOLF SPIDER
*Lycosa australicola* (Strand, 1913)

*Female.*

ID: Distinct black triangular marking on otherwise uniform grey abdomen. Carapace almost black with wide pale brown central band and lighter margins. ♀ c.15mm, ♂ c.12mm. Misplaced in *Lycosa* (represents undescribed Australian genus).

ECOLOGY: Open sclerophyll forests and bushland, particularly found in litter under trees. Also in coastal heathland. Burrows up to 15cm deep. Ad ♀ present throughout year, ♂ abundant from Nov–Mar.

RANGE: Known from NSW, NT, SA and WA south of 23°S Latitude.

## CORAL WOLF SPIDER
*Lycosa corallina* McKay, 1974

*Female.*

**ID:** Indistinct grey and black mottled pattern. ♀ c.25mm, ♂ c.20mm. Misplaced in *Lycosa* (represents undescribed Australian genus).

**ECOLOGY:** Habitat specialist in coral shingle on offshore islands. Most numerous near shoreline, possibly due to higher abundance of food around seaweed. Ad ♀ occurs throughout year, mating apparently restricted to Jul–Aug.

**RANGE:** Currently known from Houtman Abrolhos Islands and Rosemary Island (Dampier Archipelago) in northern WA.

## SALT LAKE WOLF SPIDER
*Lycosa salifodina* McKay, 1976

*Female.*

ID: Carapace uniformly grey to brown. Abdomen with indistinct chevrons and pairs of paler spots: ♀ c.25mm, ♂ c.20mm. Can be mistaken for salt lake-dwelling spiders in genus *Tetralycosa*, but with very different genitalia. Misplaced in *Lycosa* (represents undescribed Australian genus).

ECOLOGY: Surface of salt lakes, where it constructs vertical burrows or burrows that are offset at base and up to 45cm deep, generally to level where groundwater present.

RANGE: Salt lakes in WA, SA and NT.

**SHUTTLECOCK WOLF SPIDER**
*Mainosa longipes* (L. Koch, 1878)

*Female.*

ID: Dark brown to black. Median pale band on carapace and distinct cream to white transverse lines on abdomen. ♀ c.12mm, ♂ c.9mm.

ECOLOGY: *Acacia* woodland and mallee on red clay to sandy soils. Open burrow with palisade of *Acacia* phyllodes or elongated leaves reminiscent of badminton shuttlecock. Possibly reproductively active only in winter

RANGE: WA south of 25°S latitude and southern SA.

## GREY WOLF SPIDER
*Portacosa cinerea* Framenau, 2017

*Female.*

**ID:** Large. Uniform grey, sometimes with two dark, small marks centrally on abdomen. Underside uniform yellow-brown. ♀ c.20mm, ♂ c.15mm.

**ECOLOGY:** Generally open habitats, incl grasslands and open sclerophyll forests and bushlands in compacted soils. Also parks and road verges. Permanent burrow up to 20cm deep closed with trapdoor. In temperate regions ad generally found in summer and autumn.

**RANGE:** South-eastern Australia, from south-eastern Qld into south-eastern SA. Common in Tas.

# CARPET WOLF SPIDER

*Tapetosa darwini* Framenau, Main, Harvey and Waldock, 2009

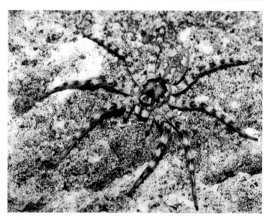

*Female.*

ID: Dorsoventrally flattened with mottled colouration and annulated legs. ♀ c.25mm, ♂ c.22mm. Can be mistaken for Huntsman Spider (Sparassidae), but has very different eye pattern.

ECOLOGY: Inhabits granite outcrops, where hides under exfoliating rock slabs during day and emerges at night to hunt. Reproductively active in late spring/early summer.

RANGE: South-western WA.

# GARDEN WOLF SPIDER
*Tasmanicosa godeffroyi* (L. Koch, 1865)

*Female.*

ID: Union-Jack carapace pattern of radiating lines (characteristic for *Tasmanicosa*). Abdomen with chevron pattern. Underside of carapace and abdomen black. ♀ c.22mm; ♂ c.18mm. Accurate ID of 17 similar Australia *Tasmanicosa* species requires microscope.

ECOLOGY: Dry, open sclerophyll forests, in particular where disturbed or near clearings. Not uncommon in parks, gardens and agricultural landscapes. Permanent burrow up to 20cm deep. In temperate zones ♀ reproductively active from Nov–Apr.

RANGE: South of c.20°S Latitude, incl Tas.

VENOM: Bite potentially painful, generally causing itchiness and redness at bite site. Venom may be fast-acting and fatal to dogs and cats.

# LEUCKART'S WOLF SPIDER
*Tasmanicosa leuckartii* (Thorell, 1870)

*Female.*

ID: Union-Jack carapace pattern of radiating lines (as all *Tasmanicosa*). Abdomen with chevron pattern. Underside of carapace black, underside of abdomen black with species-specific pale central patch. ♀ c.25mm, ♂ c.20mm.

ECOLOGY: Variety of forest and bushland habitats to semi-arid grasslands and paddocks. More common than other *Tasmanicosa* in floodplains or near permanent or ephemeral waterbodies. Shallow burrow of up to 15cm depth, but burrow fidelity low. ♀ with eggsacs mainly from Jan–Apr.

RANGE: Very common in southern mainland Australia south of 25°S Latitude, but rarely found in Tas.

VENOM: Local pain, redness and itchiness at bite site. Systemic effects such as nausea rare.

## WOLVERINE WOLF SPIDER
*Tasmanicosa hughjackmani* Framenau and Baehr, 2016

*Male.*

**ID:** Union-Jack carapace pattern of radiating lines (as in all *Tasmanicosa*). Underside of carapace and abdomen black. ♀ c.25mm, ♂ c.20mm. Very similar to *T. godeffroyi* (Garden Wolf Spider), from which differs mainly by microscopic characters of genitalia.

**ECOLOGY:** Sclerophyll forests and bushland, where constructs shallow burrow among leaf litter. Reproductively active from spring to late summer.

**RANGE:** Common in Vic and south-eastern SA.

**VENOM:** Unknown, but effects believed to be similar to *T. godeffroyi* (Garden Wolf Spider).

## BAUDINETTE'S SALT LAKE WOLF SPIDER
*Tetralycosa baudinettei* Framenau and Hudson, 2017

ID: ♀ with grey carapace and abdomen and darker discolourations. ♂ carapace dark brown and abdomen grey to olive-grey and sometimes with indistinct heart-shaped mark. ♀ c.13mm, ♂ c.10mm. Very similar, but darker overall, to *T. alteripa* (McKay, 1976), which may occur on same salt lake.

*Female.*

ECOLOGY: Salt lakes where constructs offset burrow to depth of groundwater. Burrow may be closed, but is detectable by semicircle and pile of mud pellets. Ad ♂ and ♀ from Oct–Mar.

*Male.*

RANGE: Salt lakes around Kalgoorlie, WA. Similar *T. alteripa* found in southern WA and SA. Six further *Tetralycosa* species known from salt lakes in Australian interior.

# BEACH WOLF SPIDER
*Tetralycosa oraria* (L. Koch, 1876)

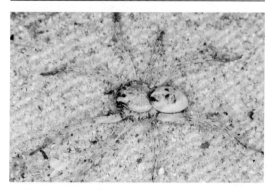

*Male.*

**ID:** Very variable colouration, from uniformly sandy-brown to dark brown with pale lines and patches. Often with indistinct pale broad lateral bands on carapace. Abdomen with arrow-shaped pale heart mark. ♀ c.12mm, ♂ c.8mm.

**ECOLOGY:** Coastal beaches and sand dunes, where may construct flimsy burrow to hide during day, otherwise nocturnal. Ads found year-round with no clear seasonal pattern of reproductivity.

**RANGE:** Coastal mainland Australia south of approximately 25°S Latitude. Also in Tas.

## ROUGH HUNTER
*Venator immansuetus* (Simon, 1909)

*Female.*

**ID:** Dark brown carapace with area behind paler head particularly dark. Abdomen with distinct chevron pattern. Abdomen underside with black patch covering front two-thirds. ♀ c.12mm; ♂ c.8mm.

**ECOLOGY:** Native woodland under dense canopy and new leaf litter or dead, flattened annual herbs. Also summer-dry swamps and wetlands and not uncommon in suburban parks and gardens. ♀ has eggsacs and juvs mainly in spring and dies by late Dec. ♂ matures from Mar–Nov, with highest reproductive activity in May.

**RANGE:** South-western WA.

**VENOM:** Reported as painful, but otherwise only minor local effects.

## SPENCER'S HUNTER
*Venator spenceri* Hogg, 1900

*Female.*

**ID:** Dark brown carapace, somewhat darker behind head region. Abdomen with distinct chevron pattern. Underside of abdomen with black patch that covers front two-thirds. ♀ c.16mm, ♂ c.10mm.

**ECOLOGY:** Dry sclerophyll forests, incl those of Black Box, Box-Ironbark, Cypress Pine, River Red Gum and Coolibah. ♂ reproductively active from Mar–Apr. ♀ constructs eggsac after winter and into early summer.

**RANGE:** South-eastern Australia, from southern Qld into SA; absent in Tas.

## KONE'S HUNTRESS
*Venatrix konei* (Berland, 1924)

*Female carrying eggsac.*

ID: Small spider with brown carapace and paler median band; abdomen mottled brown with indistinct heart mark and pairs of white spots; legs mottled. ♀ c.8mm, ♂ c.6mm.

ECOLOGY: Prefers partly-shaded, open areas close to water and often found scuttling in large numbers in mud and grass at dams. Has a wide climatic tolerance being found across all Australian climatic zones. Active at night and hides during day under rocks and in crevices. Ad from Sep–Jan.

RANGE: Throughout Australia; also in NZ and New Caledonia.

## LARGE RIVER HUNTRESS
*Venatrix lapidosa* (McKay, 1974)

*Male.*

ID: Uniformly olive-grey to brown. Underside uniformly black in ad, some pale banding under abdomen in juv. ♀ c.20mm, ♂ c.15mm.

ECOLOGY: Gravelly river banks where spiders hide under rocks during day and hunt at night. Prey may include small vertebrates such as frogs and tadpoles. In Vic, juv development lasts about 16 months and ad reproductivity occurs in spring and summer. In south-east Qld mature spiders from Jan–Apr.

RANGE: Rivers of Great Dividing Range from south-eastern Qld into eastern Vic.

# FOUR-SPOTTED HUNTRESS
*Venatrix pictiventris* (L. Koch, 1877)

*Female carrying eggsac.*

ID: Dark brown carapace with wide, pale brown median band. Abdomen with dark central chevron pattern. Underside of abdomen black with six white spots. ♀ c.10mm, ♂ c.8mm. Two *Venatrix* with similar spots under abdomen, *V. allopictiventris* Framenau and Vink, 2001 and *V. hickmani* Framenau and Vink, 2001, both limited to south-eastern Qld and northern NSW.

ECOLOGY: Open woodland and woodland ecotones, also near rivers. Often in suburban parks and gardens, where spiders roam freely in leaf litter and grass. Reproductively active in spring and summer.

RANGE: South-eastern Australia from south-eastern Qld into central-southern SA. Also Tas.

VENOM: Local effects such as redness, itchiness and minor swelling.

## EASTERN LAWN-RUNNER
*Venatrix pseudospeciosa* Framenau and Vink, 2001

*Male.*

ID: Dark brown carapace with wide, pale brown median band. Abdomen dark brown with wide pale median band that generally includes dark spindle-shaped heart mark. Underside of abdomen with two white lines. ♀ c.13mm, ♂ c.10mm. Similar *V. speciosa* (L. Koch, 1877) from south-eastern Australia and *V. esposica* Framenau and Vink, 2001 from SA and Vic.

ECOLOGY: Open habitats such as meadows, grasslands and floodplains. Most common Wolf Spider in suburban Melbourne and Adelaide, where spiders roam freely hunting prey. ♀ with eggsacs between Sep–Dec.

RANGE: South-eastern Australia from southern NSW into central-southern SA. Also Tas.

VENOM: Local effects such as redness, itchiness and minor swelling.

## WESTERN LAWN-RUNNER
*Venatrix pullastra* (Simon, 1909)

*Female with spiderlings.*

ID: Brown to dark brown carapace with pale brown median band. Abdomen mottled brown to dark brown with paler central area. ♀ c.10mm, ♂ c.7mm.

ECOLOGY: Open, wet habitats such as swamps, near lakes and rivers and in estuaries. Very common on well-watered suburban lawns, where roams freely to hunt prey. Ads seen throughout year, but ♀ with eggsac most common in Oct–Nov.

RANGE: South-western WA.

## COMMON WEB-BUILDING VENONIA
*Venonia micarioides* (L. Koch, 1877)

*Female.*

ID: Elongated shiny black Wolf Spider with small white spot at end of abdomen. Sometimes with traverse silvery lines on abdomen. ♀ c.5mm, ♂ c.4mm.

ECOLOGY: Open woodland and grassland. Constructs sheet-web with funnel retreat in vegetation or depressions in soil, such as under roots or in tracks of cattle. Densities can be very high. In temperate climates ads found in spring and summer.

RANGE: Throughout Australia, but absent from arid and semi-arid interior. Absent from tropical NT where genus represented by *V. kimjoopili*, *V. sungahae* and *V. infundibulum*.

## WANDERING GHOSTS
*Argoctenus* spp.

*Female.*

ID: Brown carapace often with pale, irregular banding. Abdomen often with dark, elongated triangular patch edged with white lines. Carapace and abdomen with tufts of setae. ♀ c.12mm, ♂ c.10mm. Taxonomy of *Argoctenus* currently unresolved and many similar species exist.

ECOLOGY: Common in vegetated habitats of all climatic zones. Mainly in leaf litter of open to closed forests and bushland; also parks and gardens.

RANGE: Genus *Argoctenus* occurs Australia-wide; species-level distribution patterns currently unresolved.

*Male.*

# COMMON PROWLING SPIDER
*Mituliodon tarantulinus* (L. Koch, 1873)

*Male.*

ID: Mottled brown to black carapace. Abdomen uniformly brown with pairs of indistinct spots. Underside of abdomen black with white spots. ♀ c.20mm, ♂ c.16mm.

ECOLOGY: Free roaming, nocturnal litter-dweller in rainforests, semi-evergreen vine thickets and eucalypt forests. Hides during day under rocks and rotting logs.

RANGE: Widespread and common in Australia, incl Tas, with exception of central arid and semi-arid zone and NT.

VENOM: Bite may be painful; euphoria, dizziness and light-headedness reported.

# LARGE PROWLING SPIDERS
*Miturga* spp.

*Female.*

**ID**: Various patterns of black stripes on brown carapace. Abdomen also with striped pattern, often less distinct and dissolved into spots. ♀ c.20mm, ♂ c.16mm.

*Miturga gilva* L. Koch, 1872 and *Miturga lineata* Thorell, 1870 most common species, but field ID difficult.

**ECOLOGY**: Free roaming, nocturnal hunter in variety of vegetated habitats. May build sheet-web as retreat.

**RANGE**: Genus *Miturga* widespread and common in Australia in all climatic zones. Species-level distribution patterns currently unresolved.

**VENOM**: Due to size of spider, bite may be painful.

*Male.*

# COMMON RED-AND-BLACK SPIDER
*Nicodamus peregrinus* (Walckenaer, 1841)

*Female.*

ID: Carapace entirely red. Abdomen black. Spinnerets and surrounds red. Legs red, but terminal segments of front legs black. ♀ c.10mm, ♂ c.11mm.

ECOLOGY: Common under bark, logs and stones in forested habitats, also garden and parks. Ads primarily present from Sep–Mar.

RANGE: Mainland eastern Australia as far north as Mackay (Qld) into eastern SA, also in Tas. Very similar *N. mainae* Harvey, 1995 occurs from south-western WA into SA.

## COMMON WALL SPIDER
*Oecobius navus* Blackwall, 1859

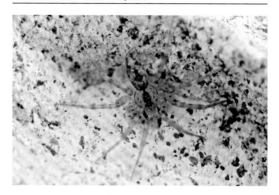

*Male.*

ID: Oval to kidney-shape carapace, generally wider than long and protruding at front. Abdomen somewhat elongated. ♀ c.4mm; ♂ c.3mm. Most common of five *Oecobius* species known from Australia, ID possible based on pattern.

ECOLOGY: Synanthropic spider known only from around buildings and walls. Construct small star-shaped mesh- or sheet-webs across cracks and corners of brick walls. Encircles prey and swathes with silk. Mating in special web constructed by ♂.

RANGE: Throughout Australia, less common in arid and semi-arid zones. Otherwise cosmopolitan.

## GRACILE LYNX SPIDER
*Oxyopes gracilipes* (White, 1849)

*Male.*

ID: Lynx Spiders have typical hexagonal eye pattern and very spiny legs. Carapace yellow-orange with three wide longitudinal brown to black stripes. Abdomen cream with brown to black markings; colouration variable overall. ♀ c.7mm, ♂ c.5mm. Many *Oxyopes* species exist in Australia, but taxonomy poorly resolved. Species-level ID difficult in field.

ECOLOGY: Diurnal sit-and-wait predator catching prey by running and jumping, on low vegetation such as shrubs, tall grass and tussocks. ♀ suspends eggsac on twigs in vegetation and guards until hatching.

RANGE: Australia-wide, but species-specific distribution pattern uncertain due to poorly known taxonomy of genus; also in NZ.

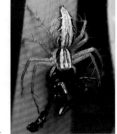

*Female.*

## COMMON DADDY LONG-LEGS
*Pholcus phalangioides* (Fuesslin, 1775)

*Female
carrying
eggsac.*

ID: Extremely long, thin legs. Elongated abdomen with indistinct darker patches. Carapace with dark central patch. ♀ c.8mm, ♂ c.7mm.

ECOLOGY: Synanthropic, very common in tangle-web in and around houses. Prey includes much larger Huntsman and Redback Spiders. As other pholcids, *Pholcus* shows maternal care with ♀ carrying loose eggsac between fangs. Often seen moving erratically in web, likely to confuse predators or help entangle prey.

RANGE: Australia-wide. Cosmopolitan.

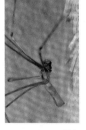

*Male.*

## NATAL DADDY LONG-LEGS
*Smeringopus natalensis* Lawrence, 1947

*Female.*

ID: Elongated abdomen and extremely long, thin legs. Abdomen with distinct pattern of white lines and darker patches. Carapace with dark median line that is narrower centrally. ♀ c.9mm, ♂ c.7mm.

ECOLOGY: Synanthropic, introduced from Africa. Less common than Common Daddy Long-legs (*P. phalangioides*) and apparently more frequently found outside than inside houses. Also locally common in parks.

RANGE: Australia-wide. More common in southern half of country.

## NORTHERN FISHING SPIDER
*Dolomedes facetus* L. Koch, 1876

*Female.*

**ID:** Yellow-brown to green. Carapace with narrow median and wide pale lateral bands. Abdomen with broad pale bands along sides and pairs of elongated short white lines. ♀ c.20mm, ♂ c.17mm.

**ECOLOGY:** Rivers, creeks and still water. Hunt at water's edge, mainly for waterborne prey, incl small vertebrates and insects that fall onto surface.

**RANGE:** Australia-wide, except south-west WA and Tas.

# UNSTEADY FISHING SPIDER
*Dolomedes instabilis* L. Koch, 1876

*Male.*

ID: Dark brown with broad white lateral bands on carapace. ♂ pedipalp femora elongated. ♀ c.25mm, ♂ c.20mm. Species ID in field difficult against other similar *Dolomedes*.

ECOLOGY: Along gravelly waterways of Great Dividing Range, where found under large rocks. Spiders mature generally in spring and summer. Like all fishing spiders, constructs nursery web for young in vegetation. A timid spider, that dives when disturbed

RANGE: East coast of Australia, from northern Qld to Vic.

# NORTHERN LINED FISHING SPIDER
*Hygropoda lineata* (Thorell, 1881)

*Female.*

ID: Elongated green to brown spider. Carapace with narrow white lines. Abdomen with elongated white spots. Legs annulated with white rings. ♀ c.11mm, ♂ c.10mm.

ECOLOGY: Horizontal, flimsy sheet-web over large leaf not far above ground. Generally near water. Prey includes mainly flies and mosquitos.

RANGE: Northern Qld, into Indonesia.

## GIANT FISHING SPIDER
*Megadolomedes australianus* (L. Koch, 1865)

*Male.*

**ID:** Brown to dark brown with white bands along side of carapace and abdomen, particularly distinct in ♂. Abdomen elongated. Very long, banded legs with span of 15cm in ♀ and 6cm in ♂. Tarsi flexible. ♀ c.25mm, ♂ c.12mm.

**ECOLOGY:** Along waterways on or under logs and rocks. Mature ♂ only in Nov–Dec. Preys on aquatic insects, also takes small vertebrates incl fish. Despite size timid and dives when disturbed.

**RANGE:** East coast, from northern Qld to Tas.

# BASKING JUMPING SPIDER
*Apricia jovialis* (L. Koch, 1879)

*Female.*

ID: Black with characteristic orange-beige pattern on abdomen that includes two narrow bands reaching around sides. Legs from tibiae reddish-brown. ♀ pedipalps with conspicuous white setae. ♀ c.9mm, ♂ c.7mm.

ECOLOGY: Under bark or on foliage in wide range of habitats, often in and around houses and basking on sunny walls. Ads found year-round, but most common in spring and summer.

RANGE: Southern half of Australia. Along east coast into south-eastern Qld, in WA as far north as approximately Geraldton.

VENOM: Painful bite with local discolouration and swelling, systemic effects include headaches.

# YOUNG STAG JUMPER
*Canama hinnula* (Thorell, 1881)

*Male.*

ID: ♂ with bronze-brown carapace and metallic blue-green to grey abdomen. Fangs elongated and iridescent bluish-black. ♀ paler overall and lacks iridescence. ♀ c.10mm; ♂ c.9mm.

ECOLOGY: Well vegetated areas, where found in foliage and on bark of eucalypts. Otherwise ecology poorly known.

RANGE: Coastal Qld and hinterland.

VENOM: Painful bite with local discolouration and swelling, systemic effects include headaches.

## BLACK BEETLE-MIMIC
*Coccorchestes ferreus* Griswold, 1984

*Male.*

ID: Unmistakable shiny black Jumping Spider that mimics small beetle. Carapace punctuated and abdomen shiny. ♀ size unknown, ♂ c.3mm.

ECOLOGY: Low foliage of shrubs and trees. Otherwise ecology poorly known.

RANGE: Northern Qld.

## GREEN ANT-HUNTER
*Cosmophasis bitaeniata* (Keyserling, 1882)

*Female.*

**ID:** Carapace shiny bronze-brown. Abdomen orange with whitish bands and distinct black spot. ♂ and ♀ of similar colour and size. ♀ c.6mm, ♂ c.5mm.

**ECOLOGY:** Mimics cuticular hydrocarbon profile of Green Tree Ant (*Oecophylla smaragdina*). Preys primarily on larvae of host ants, typically by removing these from mandibles of worker ants. Able to avoid workers by daylight due to visual awareness.

**RANGE:** Northern Australia (NT, Qld). Also in south-east Indonesia, Papua New Guinea and Pacific islands to Fiji.

# SPARKLING NORTHERN JUMPING SPIDER
*Cosmophasis micarioides* (L. Koch, 1880)

*Female.*

*Male.*

ID: Carapace with distinct iridescent traverse bands of bluish-green and reddish-brown that reach to carapace margin. ♂ abdomen black with central blue-green band and terminal spot and lateral white bands. ♀ abdomen black with variable pattern of white lines and orange spots. ♀ c.6mm; ♂ c.6mm. Similar to *C. thalassina* (C. L. Koch, 1846) but dark carapace bands do not reach edge in that species.

ECOLOGY: Tropical vegetation such as palms. Found in silken hide-outs in crevices on leaves. ♂ employs a variety of mating displays depending on the mating status of ♀. ♂ builds silk chamber near those of imm ♀ until they mature.

RANGE: Northern Australia (NT, Qld). Also Papua New Guinea.

**BEARDED JUMPING SPIDER**
*Cytaea severa* (Thorell, 1881)

*Male.*

ID: Indistinctly mottled grey with bushy setae below eyes and on chelicerae. ♂ with red discolouration around eyes. Abdomen with longitudinal, irregular dark lines. ♀ c.7mm, ♂ c.7mm.

ECOLOGY: Free-hunter in variety of habitats. Found also near human habitation. Ecology otherwise poorly known.

RANGE: Tropical Qld south to Sydney. Sporadically found in WA, but poor taxonomy in genus *Cytaea* makes interpretation of distribution difficult. Also reported from NZ.

# BRONZE AUSSIE JUMPER
*Helpis minitabunda* (L. Koch, 1880)

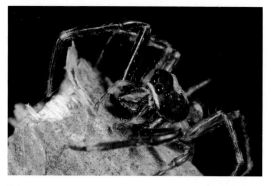

*Male.*

ID: Elongated and mottle pale to dark brown. Fringe of white setae under eyes. Carapace with broad paler central band, more conspicuous in ♂. ♂ darker overall than ♀ with long, dark first pair of legs. ♀ c.10mm, ♂ c.11mm.

ECOLOGY: Free-hunting with broad habitat tolerance. Common in garden, parks and around houses.

RANGE: Eastern Australia from tropical Qld to Adelaide, incl Tas. Also NZ.

# FLAT JUMPING SPIDERS
*Holoplatys* spp.

ID: Elongated with flattened carapace and abdomen. Many species variable in colour and pattern; often indistinctly black, brown or grey. Some species mimic ants. ♀ c.4–11mm, ♂ c.2–8mm. ID of 36 Australian *Holoplatys* species difficult due to poor taxonomic resolution.

ECOLOGY: Free-hunting spiders often seen on trees, hiding in crevices and under bark. Common around houses, hiding in narrow gaps of fences and brickwork.

RANGE: Throughout Australia in all climatic regions. Species-level distribution patterns difficult to judge as many species known only from limited number of specimens.

# RED-HEADED HOUSE HOPPER
*Hypoblemum albovittatum* (Keyserling, 1883)

*Female.*

ID: ♂ with field of orange-red setae in eye region, abdomen covered in long grey-brown setae, thinner in centre. ♀ with dark eye region surrounded by ring of pale setae. ♀ c.8mm, ♂ c.7mm.

ECOLOGY: Free-hunting. Most commonly observed around houses and gardens. Also in other open habitats, such as gravelly river banks and road verges.

RANGE: Eastern Australia, mainly reported from in and around cities.

*Male.*

## PEACOCK SPIDERS
*Maratus* spp.

*Undescribed* Maratus *female.*

ID: Extraordinary, species-specific colour variations on abdomen of ♂ (some illustrated here). ♂ also with flaps and/or fringes of variable shape and colour on sides of abdomen, which are extended during courtship display. ♀ generally inconspicuous brown shades.
♀ c.3–6mm, ♂ c.2–5mm.
Currently more than 70 *Maratus* species described in Australia, some likely misattributed to genus, but still many undescribed species expected.

Maratus pavonis *male.*

# SALTICIDAE

*Right:* Maratus chrysomelas
male.

*Below:* Maratus mungaich
group male.

*Opposite above and below:*
Undescribed Maratus *male.*

ECOLOGY: Free-hunting spiders in all habitats, incl extreme habitats such as salt lakes and beaches. ♂ exhibits elaborate mating dance by extending abdomen and stretching ornamented third pair of legs when courting ♀.

RANGE: Throughout Australia. Some species with very wide distributions, others known only from single locality.

# NORTHERN GREEN JUMPING SPIDER
*Mopsus mormon* Karsch, 1878

*Male.*                    *Female.*

ID: Unmistakable green with two dark narrow lines along abdomen. ♂ with brown and black in head region and fangs. Sides of head region with distinct fringe of white setae. ♀ often green with white and red lines and spots between eyes. Abdomen sometimes brown. ♀ c.13mm, ♂ c.13mm.

ECOLOGY: Rainforests, hunting on green foliage. Also garden and parks. ♀ constructs silk retreats between leaves. Complex mating behaviour of ♂ that differs depending on receptivity of ♀.

RANGE: Northern Australia, along east coast to northern NSW. Also Papua New Guinea.

VENOM: Can inflict painful bite, but systemic effects rare.

# ANT-MIMICKING JUMPING SPIDERS
*Myrmarachne* spp.

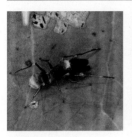

BOTH ABOVE: *Male.*

ID: Small, elongated and large variety of forms and colours, all mimicking ants. ♂ often with elongated, protruding fangs. ♀ c.5mm, ♂ c.5mm. Currently 13 species of *Myrmarachne* described in Australia, mainly from east, but likely many more species present.

ECOLOGY: Apparently mimic ants mainly to avoid predation (Batesian mimicry), as spiders generally don't prey on ants. Spiders display transformational mimicry, i.e. mimic different ant models at different stages as they mature. Otherwise ecology poorly known, but found in all climatic zones in Australia

RANGE: Australia-wide.

*Female.*

129

# CAST-IRON JUMPER
*Omoedus metallescens* (L. Koch, 1879)

Male.

ID: Black with distinct pattern of white lines and patches on abdomen. ♂ with distinct orange legs. ♀ c.10mm, ♂ c.10mm.

ECOLOGY: An apparent rainforest species, but ecology poorly known.

RANGE: Known from tropical northern Australia (WA to Qld), on east coast as far south as Townsville.

Female.

130

## MASSIVE GARDEN JUMPER
*Opisthoncus quadratarius* (L. Koch, 1867)

*Male.*

ID: Brown to black overall with pale central line along abdomen. ♂ with large patch of white setae behind eyes. ♀ abdomen paler than that of ♂ and white line accompanied by white patches. ♀ c.13mm, ♂ c.12mm.

ECOLOGY: Open, well-vegetated habitats. Common in parks and gardens. Ecology otherwise poorly known.

RANGE: Currently known from Qld and NSW.

# OPISTHONCUS JUMPER
*Opisthoncus* spp.

Female.

Male.

ID: Variable colouration, but generally with dark spot ('false eye') between posterior eyes. ♀ c.6–13mm, ♂ c.4–12mm. Currently 30 species described in Australia, but no recent taxonomic treatment. Many undescribed species.

ECOLOGY: Variety of vegetated habitats, but particularly common in parks and gardens. Species-level ecology poorly known.

RANGE: Most states. Apparently absent from arid central Australia and tropical far north. Species-level distribution patterns unknown due to poorly resolved taxonomy.

# FRINGED JUMPER
*Portia fimbriata* (Doleschall, 1859)

BOTH PHOTOS: *Female.*

ID: Characteristic tufts of setae over body incl legs. ♂ dark brown to black with white line in middle of carapace and white patches on sides. Pedipalps with white setae. ♀ cryptically mottled brown. ♀ c.10mm, ♂ c.8mm.

ECOLOGY: Tropical rainforests. *Portia* well known for adaptable predatory behaviour that has been interpreted as learning – unique within spiders. Prefers other spiders as prey and uses prey capture webs (unusual in Jumping Spiders), invades other spiders' webs (by producing deceptive signals on web), or cryptically stalks its prey and freezes if it perceives to have been detected.

RANGE: Tropical Australia as far south as Cairns. Also from India into South-East Asia.

*Male.*

133

## COMMON SPITTING SPIDER
*Scytodes thoracica* (Latreille, 1802)

*Male.*

ID: Six eyes. Yellow-brown with characteristic pear-shaped carapace that is distinctly lower in head region than towards back. Species-specific black lyre-shaped pattern on carapace and irregular spots on abdomen. ♀ c.6mm, ♂ c.5mm.

ECOLOGY: Synanthropic, mainly found in and around houses. Specialised prey capture behaviour involves spitting venomous gluey silk from specialised glands in fangs in zig-zag pattern at high speed across prey, which is pinned down and paralysed at same time.

RANGE: Australia-wide. Less common in arid centre.

## JARRAH FLATTIE
*Karaops jarrit* Crews and Harvey, 2011

*Male.*

ID: Flattened shape. Pale brown with mottled darker colouration. ♀ c.6mm, ♂ c.5mm. Often mistaken for small Huntsman Spider (Sparassidae), but very different eye pattern of 6 + 2 (Sparassidae 4 + 4). ID of 37 described *Karaops* species generally requires microscopic investigation of genitalia.

ECOLOGY: Very fast-running spiders under bark and exfoliating rocks of granite outcrops. Summer-mature.

RANGE: South-western WA.

## SOCIAL HUNTSMAN SPIDER
*Delena cancerides* Walckenaer, 1837

*Male.*

ID: Grey-brown overall. May have indistinct darker patches on abdomen. Two front pairs of legs distinctly longer than two rear pairs. ♀ c.30mm+, ♂ c.25mm.

ECOLOGY: Common bark-dwelling spider on dead trees, but ventures into houses. ♀ and offspring (often hundreds) found in social groups. Colony retains multiple clutches of offspring until sexually mature at about 1 year of age. Single ad daughter will take over colony retreat after mother's death.

RANGE: Southern Australia, as far north as about Perth, WA, and Rockingham, Qld. Introduced to NZ.

VENOM: Bites rare but painful due to size of spider. Pain short-lived and very rarely mild systemic effects such as headache and nausea.

# TROPICAL HUNTSMAN SPIDER
*Heteropoda venatoria* (Linnaeus, 1767)

*Male.*  *Female.*

ID: ♂ with dark carapace, paler around margins and eyes. Band of pale setae under eyes. Abdomen variably spotted with central dark heart mark. ♀ less distinct than ♂. ♀ c.25mm, ♂ c.22mm; one of 41 described species of *Heteropoda* in Australia.

ECOLOGY: Tropical and subtropical foliage and litter. Also parks and gardens. ♀ carries eggsac under body.

RANGE: Northern tropical, mainly coastal Australia, south to Brisbane. Very rare in temperate zones. Otherwise pantropical.

VENOM: Local generally short-lived pain, rarely mild systemic effects such as headache and nausea.

## MURRAY RIVER HUNTSMAN SPIDER
*Holconia murrayensis* Hirst, 1991

*Male.*

ID: Dark brown carapace with pale edges and cross-shaped central pattern. Abdomen mottled dark brown. Legs pale with darker spots. ♀ c.35mm, ♂ c.32mm. One of a number of similar species of *Holconia* in Australia.

ECOLOGY: Often under bark of River Red Gum (*Eucalyptus camaldulensis*). Ads found throughout year.

RANGE: Along Murray River floodplain in Vic, NSW and SA.

VENOM: Local, generally short-lived pain, rarely mild systemic effects such as headache and nausea.

# DIANA'S BADGE HUNTSMAN SPIDER

*Neosparassus diana* (L. Koch, 1875)

*Female.*

ID: Less flattened than many other Huntsman Spiders. Uniform orange-brown. Underside of abdomen with central black 'badge' adorned with pair of white spots. ♀ c.22mm, ♂ c.17mm. One of about 20 species of Australian *Neosparassus* with poorly known taxonomy.

ECOLOGY: Nocturnal under loose bark, among foliage or under loose stones. Also around houses on fences and walls. Eggsac circular, cushion-shaped and fixed under bark – constructed in late spring to early summer.

RANGE: Very common in south-eastern Australia into south-eastern Qld. Few records from south-western WA.

VENOM: Painful due to size of spider, but pain short-lived and very rarely mild systemic effects.

# LICHEN HUNTSMAN SPIDER
*Pandercetes gracilis* L. Koch, 1875

*Male.*

ID: Unmistakable, highly cryptic and hairy Huntsman Spider in pale to dark shades of green. ♀ c.14mm, ♂ c.12mm. Single representative of genus in Australia.

ECOLOGY: Tropical to subtropical climates. On rainforest trees mimicking lichen on bark. Otherwise ecology poorly known.

RANGE: Eastern Qld. Also Indonesia and Papua New Guinea.

VENOM: Unknown, possible mainly localised effects such as pain, swelling, redness which will disappear quickly.

## SOMBRERO SPIDER
*Stiphidion facetum* Simon, 1902

*Female.*  *Male.*

**ID:** Mottled brown with distinct rings on long and slender legs. Abdomen with tufts of setae along two parallel white lines. Both eye rows recurved, i.e. eyes on side situated behind central ones. ♀ c.9mm, ♂ c.7mm.

**ECOLOGY:** Constructs sheet-web resembling sombrero or wide inverted funnel underneath variety of overhanging structures such as logs, rock faces or clay banks. Also in dark rooms of houses such as cellars. Spider rests at top of central part of funnel waiting for prey.

**RANGE:** South-eastern Australia from south-eastern Qld to Tas and into SA. Introduced NZ.

## HUMPED SILVER ORB-WEAVER
*Leucauge dromedaria* (Thorell, 1881)

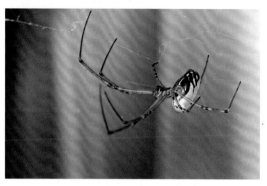

*Female.*

ID: Silvery abdomen has longitudinal black bands and traces of yellow. Underside of abdomen brown with yellowish spots or bands. Femora of legs often greenish. ♀ c.12mm, ♂ c.7mm.

ECOLOGY: Rebuilds web every day. Web slants at about 20–45° from horizontal. Spider hangs upside-down, generally in low vegetation.

RANGE: Most common along east coast and possibly in south-west WA, but taxonomy of genus poorly resolved. Also NZ.

# COMMON LONG-JAWED SPIDER
*Tetragnatha nitens* (Audouin, 1826)

*Male.*

ID: Elongated with extremely long and gaping fangs. ♀ c.12mm, ♂ c.10mm. One of 25 currently described Australian species in genus *Tetragnatha*. Species-level ID may require microscopic investigation, namely pattern of teeth on chelicerae.

ECOLOGY: *Tetragnatha* typically inhabit riparian habitats, i.e. build slanted orb-webs in vegetation over waterbodies, targeting emerging aquatic insects. When disturbed hides appressed to vegetation, incl narrow sedges, with all legs extended. Fangs of ♂ and ♀ locked together during mating to avoid aggression between pair.

RANGE: Australia-wide, generally by permanent water. Otherwise cosmopolitan, especially common in tropics.

## WESTERN COMB-FOOTED SPIDER
*Achaearanea* sp.

*Female.*

ID: Globular abdomen with characteristic red markings in back half. ID as *Achaearanea* tentative – a number of similar species appear to exist in Australia. ♀ c.4mm, ♂ c.3mm.

ECOLOGY: Common in variety of low vegetation in coastal areas or sclerophyll woodlands and forests.

RANGE: This colour form of *Achaearanea* is common in south-western WA, and probably much more widely distributed.

# DEW-DROP SPIDER
*Argyrodes antipodianus* O. Pickard-Cambridge, 1880

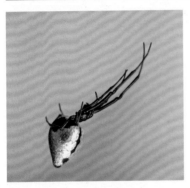

*Female.*

ID: ♀ with silvery, cone-shaped abdomen that is higher than long and tapering at top. ♂ abdomen conical/triangular and carapace with characteristic 'double-head'. ♀ c.3mm, ♂ c.2.5mm.

ECOLOGY: Congregates in small foraging groups around webs of larger Orb-weaving Spiders, where it feeds kleptoparasitically by stealing wrapped-up food from host, eating small ignored prey caught in host's web, and feeding with host on its wrapped and partially digested food bundle. In Australia predominantly found in orb-webs of *Nephila*.

RANGE: Throughout Australia. Also New Caledonia and NZ.

## BLACK CHIKUNIA

*Chikunia nigra* O. Pickard-Cambridge, 1880

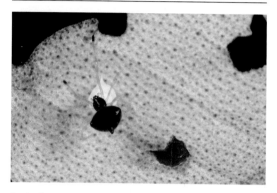

*Female with eggsac.*

ID: Unmistakable small black spider. ♀ with yellow legs and first tarsi black. ♂ with black legs, but yellow coxae. ♀ c.4mm, ♂ c.3mm.

ECOLOGY: Tropical forests on undersides of leaves, from where they extend single sticky silk threads to nearby vegetation that act as capture webs. May live in loose colonies of more than 100 ads. ♀ displays brood care for eggsacs and hatched young, which they feed by sharing prey. Spiderlings stay together for about four moults.

RANGE: Northern Qld; India to South-East Asia.

# COSMOPOLITAN CRYPTACHAEA
*Cryptachaea veruculata* (Urquhart, 1886)

*Female.*

ID: Globular abdomen with central arrow-shaped dark marking and reddish-brown patches to sides. Many other similar species in Australia. ♀ c.5mm, ♂ c.3mm.

ECOLOGY: Common on variety of substrates, often under stones and logs, where spiders found in typical cobweb. Often abundant in disturbed habitats like gardens and parks. Also on walls.

RANGE: Southern half of Australia (as far north as Perth, WA, and Brisbane, Qld), incl Lord Howe Island, Norfolk Island and Tas. Also NZ. Introduced to England and Belgium.

## ANT-EATING THERIDIID
*Euryopis* spp.

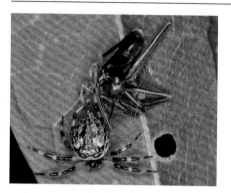

*Female.*

**ID:** Elevated head region of carapace. Abdomen longer than wide and tapering to back. Abdomen often with dark central markings but variable in colour. Front legs characteristically pointing sideways (laterigrade). Many species – ID requires microscopic examination. ♀ c.4mm, ♂ c.4mm.

**ECOLOGY:** Species in this genus are ferocious ant-hunters and often overcome prey much larger than themselves.

**RANGE:** Genus occurs Australia-wide in all sorts of vegetated habitats.

# REDBACK SPIDER
*Latrodectus hasseltii* Thorell, 1870

*Immature female.*

ID: ♀ dark brown to black with red longitudinal stripe on back of abdomen and hourglass-shaped red spot on underside. Juv often with white banding. ♂ much smaller with white stripes on abdomen, but also reddish hour-glass spot underneath. ♀ c.10mm, ♂ c.3mm.

ECOLOGY: Lives in untidy cobweb with gum-foot threads fixed to ground. Particularly common in dark areas in and around houses and sheds, but also found in natural habitats (sclerophyll forests and into deserts) under logs and other crevices.

**RANGE:** Australia-wide. Possibly spread by human activity from source population in SA. Introduced NZ and Japan.

**VENOM:**
Although not aggressive, bites occur frequently due to synanthropic tendency. Venom considered dangerous to humans due to presence of alpha-latrotoxin (neurotoxin). Can cause very strong pain, redness and swelling potentially followed by nausea, vomiting, chest pain and headache. Antivenom available.

*Male.*

*Female.*

# CUPBOARD SPIDER
*Steatoda grossa* (C.L. Koch, 1838)

*Male.*      *Female.*

**ID:** Shiny dark brown to black with creamy-white markings on abdomen. Often wrongly identified as Redback Spiders, but *Steatoda* lack red dorsal stripe and red hourglass marking under abdomen. ♀ c.9mm, ♂ c.7mm.

**ECOLOGY:** Synanthropic, i.e. mainly in and around human habitation, where constructs untidy cobwebs with gum-foot lines in dark localities. Often under or in furniture, car tyres, compost bins and worm farms.

**RANGE:** Introduced to Australia, where mainly known from southern half of country. Otherwise cosmopolitan. Very similar *S. capensis* Hann, 1990 was introduced from South Africa and has a similar distribution and habitat preferences. Both species also found in NZ.

**VENOM:** Bites medically significant, with reported moderate to severe local and radiating pain, blistering and overall unwellness that may last for several days.

## BLACK-SPOTTED THWAITESIA
*Thwaitesia nigronodosa* (Rainbow, 1912)

*Female protecting eggs.*

ID: Beautifully coloured spider with raised abdomen that has silvery patchwork of guanocytes around sides. Variable colour pattern on top, often with red or yellow shades. Generally with distinct black tubercles of varying size. ♀ c.6mm, ♂ c.5mm.

ECOLOGY: Forests and forest margins, often near creeklines. Found in small tangled web under leaves.

RANGE: East-coast, from northern Qld to Sydney, NSW.

# GREEN TREE ANT-MIMIC
*Amyciaea albomaculata* (O. Pickard-Cambridge, 1874)

*Female.*

**ID:** Green to brown elevated carapace and bright green abdomen adorned with two black spots at back. Legs rusty brown, long and thin. ♀ c.4mm, ♂ c.3mm.

**ECOLOGY:** Closely associated with Green Tree Ant or Weaver Ant (*Oecophylla smaragdinea*), which it mimics and preys upon. Black spots on back of abdomen resemble the eyes of the ants. Spider will often attack ants while hanging from silk thread as security line.

**RANGE:** Tropical northern Australia (Qld, NT, WA).

## ROSY FLOWER SPIDER
*Australothomisus rosea* (L. Koch, 1875)

*Female.*

ID: Green carapace and legs. Abdomen white with central white band that is centrally bulging towards sides with reddish-brown colouration. ♀ c.6mm, ♂ c.3mm.

ECOLOGY: Not very commonly collected and therefore ecology poorly known. Most likely found on flowers of red and white colouration for camouflage.

RANGE: Eastern Australia, currently known from Qld to Tas.

**BLACK CRAB SPIDER**
*Cymbacha saucia* L. Koch, 1874

*Female.*

ID: Domed dark brown to black carapace that is centrally marbled beige. Abdomen about as wide as long and with central olive-grey to grey sigillae surrounded by distinct narrow banding. ♀ c.7mm, ♂ c.6mm. Similar to other *Cymbacha* in Australia and taxonomy without modern treatment.

ECOLOGY: In variable vegetation where spiders hide in nest made of a folded leaf. Prey may be much larger than spider and includes ants.

RANGE: Eastern Australia from Qld to Vic.

# BIRD-DROPPING CRAB SPIDER
*Phrynarachne* spp.

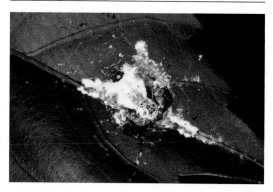

*Female.*

**ID:** Mottled white colouration and irregular carapace and abdomen shape that mimic bird droppings. ♀ c.8mm, ♂ c.5mm. Although this genus is known to occur in Australia, as yet no species has been formally described.

**ECOLOGY:** Rests on nest of white silk on or under leaf. Silk appears to exude smell of bird droppings, attracting insects such as flies to feed on excrement. The spider then preys on these insects.

**RANGE:** Tropical northern Australia (Qld, NT, WA).

# CRYPTIC CRAB SPIDERS
*Stephanopis* spp.

*Female.*

ID: Highly cryptic. Generally shades of brown with narrow part of head protruding from carapace. ♀ c.9mm, ♂ c.5mm. ID of 27 Australian *Stephanopis* species difficult due to lack of modern taxonomic revision.

ECOLOGY: *Stephanopis* are common, generally bark-dwelling spiders that occur in all climatic zones in Australia. Spiders may attach a variety of substrate, incl soil, litter or small rocks, to their body to enhance camouflage.

RANGE: Australia-wide in all climatic zones.

## COUNTRY CRAB SPIDER
*Tharpyna campestrata* L. Koch, 1874

*Female.*

ID: Black carapace with paler edge. Abdomen dark brown, dorsoventrally flattened with pair of pale central spots and short pale line at back. ♀ c.11mm, ♂ c.8mm. Nine Australian species described, but taxonomy of genus *Tharpyna* is poorly resolved, making species-level ID difficult.

ECOLOGY: *Tharpyna* are bark-dwellers on trees, facilitated by flat abdomen and camouflaged by brown colouration. ♀ lays eggsac under bark, otherwise ecology poorly known.

RANGE: Throughout Australia, most common in southern latitudes.

# WHITE-FOOTED THARRHALEA
*Tharrhalea albipes* (L. Koch, 1875)

*Female with eggs.*

ID: Pale brown to brown carapace. Abdomen mottled brown with characteristic dark wavy transverse line. ♀ c.6mm, ♂ c.4mm. ID of species based on original description, but specimens on which description was based are likely lost.

ECOLOGY: Found in tropical rainforests where it hunts as sit-and-wait predator on foliage. ♀ fixes eggsac under dense carpet of silk on top of leaves.

RANGE: Currently known from northern Qld.

## SPOTTED CRAB SPIDER
*Tharrhalea multipunctata* (L. Koch, 1874)

*Male.*

ID: Brown to green carapace and abdomen. Abdomen with black spots (characteristic for some *Tharrhalea*) and sometimes darker banding. ♀ c.5mm, ♂ c.3mm. Very similar to *T. evanida* (L. Koch, 1867) and *T. variabilis* (L. Koch, 1875).

ECOLOGY: Sit-and-wait predator found in flowers and other vegetation. Ad mainly collected in spring and summer.

RANGE: Common along east coast from central Qld into Vic, but also found in other states.

# WHITE CRAB SPIDER
*Thomisus spectabilis* Doleschall, 1859

 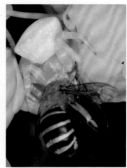

*Both female.*

ID: Colouration striking white to yellow. Head region protrudes at sides to form small conical horns. Abdomen widens towards back giving somewhat triangular appearance. ♀ c.12mm, ♂ c.5mm.

ECOLOGY: Found in a variety of habitats on white or yellow flowers, where spiders apparently have ability to adjust their colouration to some extent.

RANGE: Most common in northern half of Australia. Otherwise tropical to subtropical distribution from India to South-East Asia.

VENOM: May inflict localised pain; some systemic effect may include short-lived nausea and dizziness.

# TMARUS CRAB SPIDERS

*Tmarus* spp.

*Female.*

**ID:** Overall mottled brown. Abdomen conical, widening towards back and often abruptly truncated. ♀ c.7mm, ♂ c.5mm. Taxonomy of genus *Tmarus* in Australia has not had a modern taxonomic treatment and species-level ID is difficult.

**ECOLOGY:** Common bark- and foliage-dwelling spiders on trees and shrubs in a variety of vegetation. ♀ deposits eggsac in rolled-up leaf in vegetation.

**RANGE:** Throughout Australia, species-specific distribution patterns unresolved due to poor taxonomy.

# YELLOW-BELLIED CRAB SPIDER
*Zygometis xanthogaster* (L. Koch, 1875)

*Female.*

**ID:** White with variable brown markings on carapace and abdomen, which may be absent. Abdomen roundish. Legs often with dark brown and black rings, particularly in ♂. ♀ c.10mm, ♂ c.7mm.

**ECOLOGY:** Colour forms from white to shades of yellow, each inhabiting different plants corresponding to colour of flowers. Can change colour to some extent. In temperate Australia ads present from Sep–late Feb. ♀ builds large, flat eggsacs of fine, white silk, containing about 40 eggs.

**RANGE:** Throughout Australia. Into South-East Asia as far as Thailand.

**VENOM:** May inflict localised pain.

## MAIN'S GROUND FLATTIE
*Boolathana mainae* Platnick, 2002

*Male.*

ID: Black, flattened and with numerous brown setae on carapace and abdomen. Legs pointing sideways (laterigrade) as in many species of family. ♀ c.15mm, ♂ c.12mm. One of two species of *Boolathana* and many similar species of Trochanteriidae in Australia. ID requires examination under microscope.

ECOLOGY: Bark- and possibly litter-dwelling spider. Ads mainly found from Aug–Oct, otherwise ecology poorly known.

RANGE: South-western WA as far north as Carnarvon.

# GREY HOUSE SPIDER
*Zosis geniculatus* (Olivier, 1789)

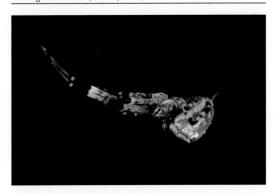

*Female.*

ID: Mottled pale grey with darker pattern. Front legs very long and thick and with distinct black and white banding on tibia. ♀ lays star-shaped eggsacs. ♀ c.8mm, ♂ c.7mm.

ECOLOGY: Build ragged circular web commonly near, under and in houses and sheds, also under bridges and other structures. Uloboridae do not have venom glands and spider overcomes prey by wrapping it.

RANGE: Northern Australia, along east coast as far south as Sydney. Otherwise pantropical.

## ANT-EATING SPIDER
*Australutica* spp.

*Female.*

ID: Black carapace. Abdomen unicoloured or with complex pattern. ♀ c.7–14mm, ♂ c.5–12mm. Taxonomy of this Australian genus is poorly resolved with many undescribed species. Species-level ID requires microscopic examination.

ECOLOGY: Some *Australutica* seem to prefer sandy habitats, e.g. near coast on sandy beaches; others occur through central deserts. Otherwise ecology poorly known.

RANGE: Australia-wide, apparently more common in central and western parts of country.

## ANT-EATING SPIDER
*Habronestes* spp.

*Female.*

ID: Black with variable patterns of yellow, orange or red spots on abdomen. ID from other similar zodariid genera generally requires examination of ♂ genitalia. ♀ c.7mm, ♂ c.5mm. Very diverse genus with currently 50 described and many more undescribed species.

ECOLOGY: Most common in semi-arid to arid environments, but known from all climatic zones in Australia. Ant-mimics that live in association with ants and prey on them. Some species have been shown to seek out prey by detecting ant alarm pheromones.

RANGE: Australia-wide.

## ANT-EATING SPIDER
*Masasteron complector* Baehr, 2004

*Male.*

ID: Black with tricoloured legs (white and black femora, other segments brown). Indistinct pair of small pale brown spots centrally on abdomen, large pale spots above spinnerets. ♂ pedipalps massive and complex. ♀ c.7mm, ♂ c.7mm. Requires ID under microscope against similar species of *Masasteron* (*M. tealei* Baehr, 2004, *M. piankai* Baehr, 2004).

ECOLOGY: Ant-mimic in shrublands and low woodland. Otherwise ecology poorly known.

RANGE: Common in western WA.

## ANT-EATING SPIDER
*Storena* spp.

*Female.*

ID: Reddish-brown to black with characteristic small, brown, pitted shield on abdomen between two, three or most often five pale spots. Carapace often darker in head region. ♀ c.10–20mm, ♂ c.8–16mm.

ECOLOGY: All climatic zones in country. As with most zodariids, *Storena* includes ant-mimics. Spiders often live in permanent burrows surrounded by palisade of leaf litter or twigs. Mature ♂ wanders in search of stationary ♀.

RANGE: Australia-wide.

# RED-HEADED MOUSE SPIDER
*Missulena occatoria* Walckenaer, 1805

ID: Raised head region and widely spaced eyes. ♂ with distinctly red head and fangs. ♀ lacks red and difficult to distinguish from other Mouse Spiders. ♀ c.20mm, ♂ c.15mm. ♂ of other *Missulena* species (e.g. *M. langlandsi* Harms & Framenau, 2013, *M. insignis* (O.Pickard-Cambridge, 1877)) have red heads, but *M. occatoria* is most widespread.

ECOLOGY: Permanent burrow with either side-shaft or double door. Wandering ♂ searches for ♀ from autumn to mid-winter. Unlike other mygalomorph spiders which are nocturnal, *Missulena* ♂ can often be seen wandering during day. Spiderlings disperse via ballooning at least for short distances.

RANGE: Australia-wide. Replaced by other red-headed Mouse Spider species (e.g. *M. langlandsi*) in north-eastern WA.

VENOM: Spiders aggressive when threatened and venom of *Missulena* chemically similar to that of Funnel-web Spiders (Hexathelidae). Bite therefore potentially dangerous, but spiders appear to mainly apply 'dry bites' in defence without major envenomation.

*Male.*

## SILVERBACK
*Idiommata blackwallii* (Cambridge, 1870)

*Male.*

ID: Variable dark brown to black carapace and abdomen and often silvery cover of setae, in particular in ♂. Feet with dense covering of tufts that allow them to climb smooth surfaces. ♀ c.30mm, ♂ c.25mm. Taxonomy of *Idiommata* poorly known and many undescribed species are present in collections.

ECOLOGY: Bushland with leaf litter cover. Lives in permanent burrow that is closed with saucer-shaped door or leaves and very difficult to detect. Spiders mature in late summer and early autumn when wandering ♂ can be found.

RANGE: *Idiommata blackwallii* was originally described from Perth, but exact distribution of species unknown due to poor taxonomic resolution of genus. *Idiommata* occurs throughout country, except Tas.

VENOM: Likely painful bite due to large size of spider, but not known to cause more than local reactions at bite site. Venom of Barychelidae has not been studied and bites are rare.

*Male of unidentified* Idiommata *from Queensland.*

## CORK-LID TRAPDOOR SPIDERS
*Conothele* spp.

*Female.*

**ID:** Grey to brown with shiny carapace and a deep U-shaped central furrow (fovea). Third pair of legs has depressed saddle on tibia. ♀ c.12mm, ♂ c.10mm. Many undescribed species of *Conothele* known from Australia, in particular from arid zone.

**ECOLOGY:** Variable habitats from seashore to central deserts. Permanent vertical burrow closed with strong lid ('cork-lid') made of soil bound together with silk. Maternal care has been observed – ♀ feeds juv regurgitated prey liquid. Small spiderlings may balloon for short distances.

**RANGE:** Throughout Australia. More common in north and rarely collected in south-west.

# CURTAIN-WEB SPIDERS
*Cethegus fugax* (Simon, 1908)

*Male.*

ID: Red-brown to brown with flat carapace that has a small central depression (fovea). Spinnerets extremely long. ♀ c.14mm, ♂ c.12mm.

ECOLOGY: Permanent burrow under logs and rocks that is adorned with curtain-web, i.e. extensive vertical sheet incorporating soil and litter. Found in dry sclerophyll eucalypt forests and bushland.

RANGE: South-western Australia from Perth Hills westwards. Exact distribution unknown due to poor knowledge of taxonomy of genus.

VENOM: Very shy spiders. No recorded bites.

## SYDNEY FUNNEL-WEB SPIDER
*Atrax robustus* O. Pickard-Cambridge, 1877

*Female.*

**ID:** Very dark brown to black with very shiny carapace and no obvious pattern. Eyes in close eye group. ♂ (as in all *Atrax*) with large conical thorn on tibia of second leg. Spinnerets long and can be seen from above. ♀ c.27mm, ♂ c.17mm.

**ECOLOGY:** Most common in moist forest areas, particularly sheltered gullies, but also in drier and flatter areas. Burrows often with weak or incomplete silk lining and with funnel entrance with irregular radiating trip lines, typically sited under rocks and logs. Also in gardens, in rockeries and between dense shrubs. ♂ wanders in search of ♀ in warmer months of year.

**RANGE:** Sydney, Central Coast and Illawarra regions and west to Blue Mountains.

**VENOM:** ♂ aggressive and with highly neurotoxic and fast-acting venom compound Robustoxin (d-Atracotoxin-Ar1) that can be fatal. Antivenom available since early 1980s. ♀ venom does not contain neurotoxin.

# SPINY TRAPDOOR SPIDER
*Arbanitis* spp.

*Female.*

ID: Black to brown hairy Trapdoor Spiders, often with golden shine. Eyes in square or rectangle. ♀ c.20–35mm, ♂ c.15–25mm. Species-level ID of 63 Australian species requires microscopic examination. Many more species expected to be identified.

ECOLOGY: Permanent, generally open burrows without trapdoors, sometimes entrance raised from ground. Often found in large numbers in rainforests, sclerophyll forests, parks and gardens.

RANGE: Genus has wide distribution in eastern Australia, from central-eastern Qld south to Tas and into south-eastern SA. Particularly common in NSW.

# GIANT SPINY TRAPDOOR SPIDER
*Gaius villosus* Rainbow, 1914

*Male.*

ID: Carapace very dark brown to black and shiny. ♀ abdomen dark grey with darker median band and few setae. ♂ abdomen black and very hirsute. Eye group trapezoid. ♀ c.35mm, ♂ c.30mm. *Gaius* includes a number of additional undescribed species.

ECOLOGY: Mulga and *Acacia* groves of sclerophyll woodland. Permanent burrow with thin lid adorned by *Acacia* leaves in radial fashion. ♀ reported to be very long lived (40+ years).

RANGE: South-western and central WA. Species-level distribution of *Gaius* poorly known due to lack of taxonomic studies.

**VENOM:** Bite potentially very painful, but spider rarely encountered outside burrow. Not reported to cause more than local effects.

*Burrow.*

## SHIELD-BACKED TRAPDOOR SPIDER
*Idiosoma nigrum* Main, 1952

*Female.*

ID: ♀ with distinct rugose and hardened abdomen, somewhat truncated at back and with four circular sigillae. ♂ also rugose, but overall less sclerotised. Eye group trapezoid. ♀ c.25mm, ♂ c.22mm. More than a dozen Australian rugose or Shield-backed Trapdoor Spider species in genus *Idiosoma* and ID may require detailed examination of sclerotisation patterns (♀) and genitalia (♂).

ECOLOGY: Eucalypt woodlands among litter. Constructs permanent burrow with thin trapdoor decorated in radial pattern with eucalypt leaves and sometimes pieces of bark. Sclerotised abdomen believed to protect from desiccation and provides protection against intruders of burrow as it seals against constriction in burrow. Only spider species currently under Federal protection (listed as Vulnerable under the Environmental Protection and Biodiversity Conservation Act).

RANGE: Only known from northern WA Wheatbelt in isolated pockets of remnant vegetation.

VENOM: May behave aggressively when disturbed but no serious consequences of bite known.

Burrow.

# BLACK WISHBONE SPIDER
*Aname mainae* Raven, 2000

*Male.*

ID: Black, often with silver or golden shine. Spinnerets long, visible from above. ♀ c.25mm, ♂ c.20mm. Many similar undescribed species in genus; species-level ID difficult.

ECOLOGY: Forked Y-shaped burrow (hence 'Wishbone' Spider) with two open entrances in leaf litter. Dry sclerophyll forests and semi-arid bushland. ♂ becomes reproductively active in early to late summer, and with sufficient humidity to autumn.

RANGE: South-western WA and possibly into SA. Other records outside this range likely refer to similar black *Aname* species.

VENOM: ♂ often aggressive when disturbed and may induce painful bite. Bites of other *Aname* species have caused systemic effects.

# TEPPER'S TRAPDOOR SPIDER
*Aname tepperi* (Hogg, 1902)

*Male.*

**ID:** Densely covered with shiny bronze setae. Eyes in small group at front of carapace. Spinnerets long, visible from above. ♀ c.30mm, ♂ c.22mm.

**ECOLOGY:** Deep, sinuous burrow with oblique sitting chamber just below surface in litter of variable sclerophyll vegetation types, such as eucalypt forests and bushlands. Also in semi-arid and arid zone.

**RANGE:** South-western WA into and across southern SA, but may represent different species across this range.

**VENOM:** ♂ aggressive and may induce painful bite. Bites of other *Aname* species have caused systemic effects such as nausea and headache.

183

## QUEENSLAND WHISTLING TARANTULA
*Phlogius crassipes* (L. Koch, 1874)

*Male.*

ID: Hirsute brown Trapdoor Spider. Leg femora and tarsal segments sometimes darker. Front legs thicker than hind legs. Spinnerets long, visible from above. ♀ c.90mm, ♂ c.70mm.

ECOLOGY: Permanent, relatively shallow burrow up to 2m long, often started under rocks and logs. Rainforest gullies or cool, sheltered spots in open forests. Can produce hissing sound when provoked. Thick pads on legs allow spider to run up smooth surfaces. Popularity as pet poses conservation risk.

RANGE: East-coastal Qld and hinterland.

VENOM: Can be aggressive when handled. Painful bite but effects generally local at bite site. Bites fatal to cats and dogs.

## FOELSCHE'S TARANTULA
*Selenotholus foelschei* Hogg, 1902

*Male.*

**ID:** Hirsute, brown overall. Front and hind legs of similar size. Spinnerets long, visible from above. ♀ c.70mm, ♂ c.50mm.

**ECOLOGY:** Deep vertical burrow with open entrance and slightly raised, silk-covered rim. Inside of burrow thickly covered with silk.

**RANGE:** WA and NT.

**VENOM:** Likely painful bite with only local effects. Possibly fatal to cats and dogs.

# GLOSSARY

**Abdomen:** rear part of spider body.

**Annulations/annulated:** with ring-like subdivisions, in spiders often referring to colour patterns of legs.

**Apex/apical:** the tip (e.g. of an appendix)/near the tip.

**Arachnida:** class of terrestrial arthropods that includes spiders, scorpions and other orders.

**Basal:** area close to the base (e.g. of an appendix).

**Bulb:** secondary sexual organ of ♂ spiders located in the → cymbium of the → pedipalp.

**Carapace:** the upper chitinous plate of the → cephalothorax, e.g. where the eyes are located.

**Cephalothorax:** frontal part of the body.

**Chelicera:** first appendage of Chelicerata; jaw, consisting of a large basal part, the paturon, and the terminal part, the → fang.

**Chelicerata:** subphylum of invertebrates, includes the Arachnida.

**Coxa:** basal-most segment of spider leg attached to the → cephalothorax (plural: coxae).

**Cribellate:** specific type of silk that is exuded from the cribellum, a special spinning plate of some spiders situated in front of the → spinnerets.

**Cuticular hydrocarbons:** molecules on the surface of arthropods that are, amongst others, important for chemical communication/recognition.

**Cymbium:** the broadened, concave → tarsus of the ♂ pedipalp containing the → bulb (cymbial: on the cymbium) (plural: cymbia).

**Dermonecrosis:** death of skin cells due to enzymatic degradation.

**Ecotone:** transition zone between two habitats.

**Embolus:** terminal part of the ♂ → bulb accommodating the ejaculatory duct that is inserted into the ♀ → epigyne during copulation.

**Fang:** Needle-like part of the chelicerae that is used to penetrate prey and inject venom.

**Femur:** third → basal-most part of the spider leg, between the → trochanter and the → tibia (plural: femora).

**Guanocyte:** cell that accumulates guanine, one of the end products of a spider's protein metabolism; responsible for white colouration of many spiders.

**Gum-foot thread:** gluey vertical thread of a spider web connected to the ground, which on contact pulls prey up into the web.

**Hirsute:** hairy, a term avoided here as spiders do not have hair in the biological sense (only mammals do); spider hairs are → setae

**Kleptoparasite:** spiders

stealing prey from other spiders.

**Lateral:** towards/along the side of the body or an appendix.

**Laterigrade:** legs pointing sideways.

**Longitudinal:** along a spider's body.

**Metatarsus:** sixth → basal part of a spider leg, between → tibia and → tarsus (plural: metatarsi).

**Obligate:** by necessity; required.

**Palisade:** circular wall, here referring to burrow decorations of spiders.

**Patella:** fourth → basal-most part of a spider leg between → femur and → tibia (plural: patellae).

**Pedipalp:** second appendage of the Chelicerata; in ♂ spiders carrying the secondary sexual organ.

**Sclerotisation/sclerotised:** hardened part of a spider.

**Seta:** hair-like structure covering the exoskeleton of arthropods (plural: setae).

**Sigilla:** impressed darker → sclerotised spots present on upper surface of the → abdomen or on the → sternum generally marking points of muscle attachment (plural: sigillae).

**Spinnerets:** paired abdominal appendages of spiders through which silk strands are spun.

**sp./spp.:** abbreviation for species, i.e. sp. – singular and spp. – plural.

**Stabilimentum:** highly visible silk structure in the webs of some orb-weaving spiders, sometimes also including prey items.

**Sternum:** chitinous plate covering the underside of the → cephalothorax.

**Synanthropic:** living in close association with humans.

**Tarsus:** → apical-most segment of a spider leg articulated to the → metatarsus (plural: tarsi).

**Tibia:** fifth → basal-most segment of a spider leg between the → patella and → metatarsus.

**Trochanter:** second → basal-most segment of a spider leg between the → coxa and the → femur.

**Tubercle:** raised area on the chitinous exoskeleton.

**Ü–shaped:** pattern forming an Ü, i.e. an U with two spots on top, characteristic for the underside of the abdomen in the genus *Plebs*.

# INDEX

189

# INDEX

# INDEX